Cycles a

I.S.B.N. (

Dedication

For my parents, Eric and Rose May.

Also by Julia R May

My Feet and Other Animals

Walking Pembrokeshire with a Fruitcake

Walking with Offa

Pedals, Panniers and Punctures

Walking with Hadrian

I've Cycled Through There

Cycling Across England

Bicycles, Boats and Bagpipes

A Week in Provence

Bicycles, Beer and Black Forest Gateau

Dawdling Through The Dales

Cycling Through a Foreign Field

Introduction

When I first heard of the Coast and Castles Cycle Route I was a little unsure of its location. I knew from past experience that, like all Sustrans routes, it would be an interesting, well-thought-out cycle route; that it would take the cyclist safely through towns and cities and out into the countryside along cycle lanes, towpaths, minor roads, old railway tracks and purpose built cycle ways; and that it would encompass beautiful scenery, captivating villages and points of architectural and historical interest. But where precisely was it? The name 'Coast and Castles' didn't really provide many clues.

As an island nation Britain is surrounded by coastline. With a proud sea-faring past, the coast has long featured in our lives from Sir Francis Drake's defeat of the Spanish Armada to record-breaking round the world sailing adventurers, to shark fishing, to North Sea gas and oil exploration, to over-ambitious and under-intelligent holiday makers floating out to sea on lie lows or inflatable dolphins and having to be rescued by coast guards.

And as for the castles bit! Well again, British history, although fairly quiet in relation to home-soil-based conflict for the last three hundred years or so, more than made up for it in earlier times. From the passing of the Romans, through the Dark Ages, the Norman invasion, Plantagenets, Tudors and Stuarts and even up to the building of defensive Martello Towers during the time of the Napoleonic Wars, power hungry monarchs have fought bloody battles to rule the nation and subdue their opponents. The result is a small island nation dotted with castles, forts and defensive structures from the coast of Wales to the east coast of England, the Scottish Highlands to the English Channel and most areas in between. So the Coast and Castles Cycle Route could be anywhere along Britain's 11,000 miles of coastline.

But regardless of whereabouts the Coast and Castles cycle route might be, just its name drew me! It sounded like a fascinating cycle ride. Already my mind was conjuring up all the alluring possibilities on offer. Coast: sandcastles, ice cream, fish and chips. Castles: history, dungeons, tea rooms. What wasn't to appeal to the cyclist looking for her next pedalling adventure? I didn't care where this cycle route was, I just wanted to do it!

After a bit of research and the purchasing of the Sustainable Transport Coast and Castles map, it turned out, much to my delight, to be a journey from Newcastle to Edinburgh following, for much of the way, the Northumberland coast before turning inland through the Scottish Borders.

"Julia," I said to myself, "you're in for a treat."

Chapter One

"Julia," I said to myself, "you're lost!"

Getting lost on a cycling holiday is nothing new for me but usually I wait until I'm actually in the saddle before getting lost. This was a first: I was still driving to the start! With the bike, carefully packed panniers, an overnight bag, maps and other essentials such as supplies of teabags, biscuits and chocolate, carefully stowed in back of the car I had turned off the A59 onto a minor road that I thought, from past experience, would take me around the tea time traffic bottle-neck of Harrogate and Knaresborough. The trouble was that my past experience had been some time in the past and I'd got slightly mixed up. You know when you've driven a route a few times but not enough to make it a regular journey, how sometimes you can make a little wrong turning and then be utterly lost? (With me this is usually the case when driving into Manchester). The only positive thing to be said about this occasion was that at least I wasn't driving a minibus full of students from the college where I work. And so did not have to endure the jeered comments of "yeah! We're lost again," and "women drivers!" And that was just from the staff accompanying me.

The minor road I now found myself on wove between arable fields, through one tiny hamlet and continued along a progressively narrowing lane, quite clearly in the wrong direction. Hoping for a convenient junction in which to turn, I was eventually forced to execute a tight nine point turn in a field gateway with steep ditches on both sides and an oncoming tractor growing larger with each frantic turn of the steering wheel. Tractor and ditches successfully avoided, I retraced my route and rejoined the now even busier trunk road, trickling slowly into the busy spa town of Harrogate, nose to tail with half of the population of the Vale of York. Knaresborough was no less busy and I yearned for the quiet roads and country lanes of my eagerly anticipated cycling holiday.

I had plenty of time to yearn. The A1 was a slow going procession of cars, lorries and contraflows and by the time I reached the outskirts of Newcastle I was tired of sitting in the car and very hungry. I comforted myself with the thought that there was not much further to go to my accommodation that first night at Whitley Bay.

Yes, the Coast and Castles starts at Newcastle but accommodation there, although plentiful, can be pricey. On enquiring I had found that no guest houses or hotels in the city were keen to allow me to leave my car there for a few days. So instead I had adapted my plans and found a guest house at Whitley Bay more than happy for me to leave my car parked on their drive, and what's more they did not want to charge me for the privilege!

So my plan was to start the cycle ride at Whitley Bay the following morning, finish just to the north of Edinburgh at North Queensferry (to satisfy a desire to cycle over the Firth of Forth) and return by train to Newcastle some five days later, from where I would cycle the fourteen miles out along the start of the

6

route to my car at Whitley Bay before driving home that evening. The timings worked, the daily mileages worked and the accommodation breakdown worked too. And so, as I crept ever closer to my destination I was looking forward to a pleasant evening in a traditional seaside B&B, maybe some fish and chips for supper whilst sitting on the prom and then a sunset stroll along the beach before a good night's sleep and a full English breakfast to start me on my cycling holiday. Dream on girl!

As I reached the far side of Newcastle the traffic began to ease and by the time I was driving along the seafront into Whitley Bay there seemed to be hardly anyone around. A lone pensioner walking his border terrier shuffled slowly along the promenade; a teenager skate-boarded by in the other direction, flipping his board over the kerb, into the thankfully empty road, then back onto the kerb before executing a neat stop and catching the board in one hand. How did they do that? And why would you want to trust your safety to a cluster of tiny wheels stuck to the bottom of a bit of hardboard? Then again, people could say something similar (and often did) about cycling.

I slowed my own pace as I neared a likely looking side street: was this my turn off? Yes it was. Indicating my intention to turn left, despite the complete absence of any other road users, I turned down the road which took me away from the sea front, passing numerous guest houses, small hotels and bed and breakfast establishments until I spotted a sign for my accommodation that evening. Pulling into the small car park I stopped in a spot unlikely to cause any obstruction, there was only one other car parked there in any case and, climbing stiffly out, went and knocked on the door. It was quickly answered by a middle aged gentleman in jeans and a Newcastle United shirt. After brief introductions and a quick check to make sure my car wouldn't be in the way he showed me up two flights of stairs to a small single room at the front of the house.

"Breakfast is between eight and nine, no smoking anywhere in the house, en suite is through this door, tea and coffee over there and the T.V. remote has just had new batteries," he said in a rush. "And talking of which, if you'll excuse me, the match is about to start."

"Thanks," I replied, although I doubt he heard as he was already rushing down the stairs. The match in question was either about to ignite the entire house, and from the speed of his departure that did not seem unlikely, or more possibly it had something to do with eleven men in black and white stripy tops kicking a ball about.

I looked around the room, nothing fancy but clean and with plenty of milk and teabags and even a couple of biscuits. I put the kettle on, although not the television: football is not my thing. I unpacked whilst I waited for the kettle to boil. It didn't take long. I had already packed my panniers with everything I would need for the next few days and had left them in the car, bringing only an overnight bag into the guest house. The bag contained a few toiletries and clean cycling clothes for the following day. Clothes laid out, tea drunk and a couple of ginger nuts dunked and eaten, I was ready to venture out for something a little more substantial.

As I went downstairs the guest house seemed eerily quiet, was I the only guest? The sound of a football match echoed faintly from a room on the ground floor and a telephone was ringing but being ignored in a different room. Letting myself out, I set off in the direction of the sea front, reaching the empty promenade I had still not seen a soul. Whitley Bay was proving to be the seaside resort with no visitors; I half expected to see a tumbleweed blow past down the middle of the road. There didn't even seem to be any seagulls and both the pensioner and the skate boarder were long gone.

A couple of greasy spoon cafes failed to tempt me, even though by this time my stomach was growling loudly, the biscuits soon forgotten. I followed my nose to a fish and chip takeaway advertising freshly caught haddock: "still swimming this time yesterday" proclaimed a sign in the window, and took a gamble that they wouldn't now be swimming in grease.

With my hot steaming packet of haddock and chips with lashing of salt and vinegar burning my fingers, I hurried across the promenade to a shelter facing the sea. The chips were good, potatoes never having been strong swimmers, but the haddock was indeed swimming in fat, its batter soggy and unappetising. As I peeled off and rejected the soggier parts of the batter I was suddenly surrounded by seagulls. Word must have gone out up and down the coast that a person had arrived in Whitley Bay and was proceeding to regret buying fish and chips. From no gull population ten minutes previously this little seaside resort was now hosting a gull convention. The air was full of beating wings, raucous cries and flying feathers as public enemy number one battled for my supper. They could have the batter but they weren't having my chips! As I put the last piece of potato in my mouth the gulls took off as one and within seconds I was left alone with just a somewhat dishevelled pigeon pecking at the remaining scraps in front of my feet. Whitley Bay returned to its ghost town status.

With a twinge of heart burn threatening to turn into full blown indigestion, I took a stroll along the prom, watching as the sun began to sink over the houses and shops inland. The sky lit up as the setting sun shone on the mackerel clouds, providing beautiful orange and pink under-lighting. In the gathering dusk I returned through the empty streets to the guest house. A couple more cars were parked in the little car park and a taxi was just pulling away as I approached. My car was now blocked in, but that hardly mattered, providing I could get the bike out of the back in the morning it wouldn't be a problem.

A roar and prolonged cheering greeted me as I stepped through the front door. It's nice to be popular, although I suspected the greeting was more to do with Newcastle having scored a goal than my safe return. Climbing the stairs I came over all sleepy and was soon in bed, with another cup of tea and the television remote, trying to change the channels to get the news and weather forecast. New batteries the remote may well have had but nevertheless it didn't work. Draining the tea and giving up any hope of watching a weather forecast, I opened the window a fraction; the distant sound of the sea was the only noise I could hear as I drifted off to sleep.

Half an hour later I was awoken to the sound of slamming doors, a shriek of laughter and clattering high heels. What the? I checked my watch: eleven o'clock. The noise faded away and I drifted back to sleep.

A little while later and more slamming doors, more tramping feet but of a heavy male variety this time, so no high heels, and some rather bronchial coughing woke me again. What the? Turning over I managed after a while to sleep once more.

The next thing I was aware of was the slamming of car doors and revving engines. Who? What? What time was it? I checked my watch: the wrong side of midnight. It was some time before I fell asleep after that.

"Oi! Dave! Dave! You tosser!"

What? Who the hell was shouting? What time was it? A pounding started on the front door directly below my window.

"Dave, you ******!"

11

I sat up in bed. What on earth was going on? The pounding and shouting continued. Looking at my watch I discovered it was 3.30 a.m. The shouting started again, a mainly incoherent rant interspersed with all too coherent obscenities. Then another voice joined the chorus.

"Shut the **** up!"

(No it wasn't me). Although by that time I was wide awake, very indignant at being woken by the inconsiderate drunken behaviour of the yob below my window and quite ready to give him a piece of my mind.

"No you shut up!" came the drunken reply from below. "Tell Dave to let me in!"

"What do you want me to do? Shut up or tell Dave to let you in? I can't do both!"

Oh great! Now I had two drunks having an argument and one of them was a pedant! The pounding started up again, then some music blared out and a car engine started revving. Where on earth had I ended up? I asked myself.

I dared to get up and peer out of the window. Illuminated by the street lamp at the end of the drive and by the blazing security light above the front door, a young man much the worse for drink and possibly other less legal substances, was staggering and weaving about in the front garden. Peering myopically without my spectacles he appeared to be

12

wearing a pair of swimming trunks and some sort of bandage round his chest and to be bleeding from the mouth. Concerned that perhaps he was injured and not just drunk I turned away from the window, grabbed my glasses and put them on. Staring now with twenty-twenty vision I could see that he was actually wearing a pair of skimpy knickers, stockings, suspenders, high heels and, not a bandage, but a lacy bra, and with a blonde frizzy wig perched at a jaunty angle on his head and badly applied scarlet lipstick smeared down his chin. What the? Once again: where on earth had I come to?

Whitley Bay, that's where I'd come to. Whitley Bay, quiet, if not to say dead, seaside resort, or so I had thought. Whitley Bay, stag and hen night capital of the northeast! I had not known it at the time I'd chosen to spend that first night and booked my accommodation in the town but Whitley Bay was renowned for being *the* place to come for a stag or hen night to remember, or not to remember depending on how much the hens and stags in question had to drink. And this particular stag had clearly had plenty.

"Dave, please mate, I'm beggin' ya!" he wailed, before flinging his handbag at the front door.

By this time I didn't know whether I wanted the elusive Dave to let him in or keep him locked out. That was assuming of course that the cross-dressing stag was even at the right guest house!

With a final wail and a couple more expletives the stag hopped about on one leg while struggling to remove one of his ridiculous four inch high purple heels. Really they weren't a good match with the lipstick! Teetering a few paces, he then hurled the high heel after the handbag, and losing his balance in the process, spun round and collapsed face down in a flower bed. As a first aider should I be worried? He'd had a soft landing so was unlikely to have hit his head, he was face down so he was not going to choke on his vomit if he did throw up and he was now blissfully, thankfully quiet. So no, I wasn't worried. Well, I was worried he might come to and start shouting again but in the meantime as far as I was concerned he could stay there!

I closed the window and went back to bed but it was some time before I fell asleep. Not the best start to a cycling holiday but hey, at least there were no problems with my bike!

Chapter Two

When I opened the curtains that morning it was with relief that I noticed the drunk was no longer in the flower bed, there was however a blonde wig in the middle of the lawn. But of more concern to me was the car that had appeared at some point during the night and parked bumper to bumper with mine, effectively preventing me getting access to my bike. Oh well, it shouldn't be too difficult to find out who the car belonged to and ask them to move it. Or so I thought at the time.

Showered, dressed and with a cup of tea inside me I went downstairs to breakfast. The dining room was filling up fast as I entered and the owner of the guest house showed me to a little table crammed into the corner of the room near the window. This morning he was wearing another football shirt but with a different number on the back. Did he have the full team set?

"Do you know which of your guests owns the red Ford Fiesta?" I asked. "As it's blocking me in."

"I thought you were leaving your car?" he replied.

"Well, yes I am…"

"So it's not blocking you in then."

"No, it is. You see…"

"Either you need to move your car and you're blocked in, or you're leaving it here and you're not."

"No, I'm not moving it…"

"So there's not a problem then, is there?"

"Yes, there is a problem," I replied, beginning to get a bit frustrated, why wouldn't he just shut up and listen?

"What's the problem?"

"That car is so close to mine I won't be able to open the door."

"What's wrong with the passenger door?"

"Nothing. Why?" I asked, suddenly worried and imagining it had been damaged in the night.

"Well why can't you open the passenger door?"

"I can open the passenger door but how's that going to help me?"

"So you can get into the car," he replied as if it was obvious.

"I need to get the bike out of the car. I can't get it out through the passenger door, it's too big!"

"Your bike is in the car?" he asked. "Oh I see!"

"Yes…"

"Do you always put your bike in the car?"

"Er, yes."

"Something wrong with the roof is there?"

"What? No. It's just easier to have the bike in the car." What was wrong with this man? I was beginning to feel as if I had spent the night at Fawlty Towers!

"Right! Leave it with me!" And he marched off.

I half expected him to go outside and start beating the car with a sapling or cuff the waiter across the back of the head; instead he stood on a chair, clapped his hands and shouted for everyone's attention.

"Who has left their little Ford Fiesta badly and inconsiderately parked on my drive?" he shouted.

The dining room fell silent. You could have heard a cornflake drop.

"No one willing to admit it?" he asked. "This lady," he gesticulated in my direction and I felt myself reddening, "needs to retrieve her bicycle from her car. Not sure why she didn't put it on the roof, but never mind. So if the owner of the said vehicle wouldn't mind just moving it a few feet that would be much appreciated. Thank you."

The astonished guests all looked at me, I looked at my bowl of cereal and pretty soon the normal clatter and chatter of breakfast in a guest house resumed.

Every time a new guest appeared in the dining room they would be quizzed by 'Basil' about their vehicle, until one sheepish looking chap admitted ownership and hurried off to move the car. By this time I was so embarrassed I didn't know whether to thank him for moving it or pretend I had nothing to do with the car he had blocked in.

Soon nearly all the tables were full and yet more people continued to appear. Two young women looking very much the worse for a good night out came into the room and headed for first one and then the other remaining table.

"Yes? Can I help you?" asked 'Basil', appearing in a rush from the direction of the kitchen.

"We were looking for our room number," explained one of the women.

"Your room number? Have you forgotten it? It's on the front of your bedroom door."

"No, on the table," the second woman explained.

"Why would it be on the table?"

"Er, well, we thought there would be a table for each room," the first woman tentatively said.

"Oh, I see! There's not a guest house in the country that has the same number of tables as it does rooms," he stated with authority. "Just pick a table."

The two women hurriedly sat at the nearest vacant table. Other guests had, like me, being listening with some astonishment to this exchange and I heard several muttered comments about tables and rooms.

"I don't think he knows what he's talking about," said one man to the two young women when 'Basil' was safely out of earshot. "Every guest house I've stayed in has had a table for every room."

"Yeah, just ignore him," laughed another man. "He's put out 'cos Newcastle lost three nil last night!"

"Aw, man! You're jokin' like!" groaned someone at a different table. "I had money on that match."

A football conversation ensued that everyone except me contributed to. I sat quietly eating my way through what was turning out to be a rather good full English breakfast. With the last crumb of toast consumed I sat back to drink a last cup of tea and glanced out of the window only to see a seagull attacking the blonde wig as it lay on the lawn. Where was the owner I wondered? Was he one of these football fans? Was he still asleep? Or had he indeed been shouting and hollering outside the wrong guest house?

By the time I was unloading my bike from the car and strapping on the panniers, there were two seagulls fighting over the blonde wig. I left them to it and cycled off, swerving to avoid a purple high heel lying in the gutter, and returned to the sea front, turning left to join the cycle route along the promenade. Edinburgh here I come!

Whitley Bay was as quiet that morning as it had been the previous evening when I had first arrived. Two children were busy building sandcastles on the beach. The same pensioner was walking his dog. Of the skate boarder there was no sign. But evidence of the raucous stag and hen parties dotted the prom: empty beer cans, lager bottles and vodka shots rolled along the pavement blown by the sea breeze, half eaten hot dogs and kebabs were being fought over by gangs of gulls and a parked car was liberally covered in what appeared to be shaving foam. Further along I found myself swerving to avoid the regurgitated other halves of the hot dogs and kebabs. Lovely! As I narrowly missed yet another splatter of vomit I found myself wondering why some people only considered they had had a good night out if they spent a fortune, got drunk, threw up, possibly fell asleep in a flower bed and woke unable to remember much and with a throbbing hangover. That wasn't my idea of fun. Although I guess those same people would probably consider cycling two hundred and sixty miles not much fun either.

The sun was shining and reflecting on the tranquil blue sea as I set off that morning through the quiet town. Whitley Bay might now be surviving thanks mainly to its reputation as the place to go in the northeast for stag and hen parties but in more industrial times the small town had been part of the thriving coal mining area in this region. The town had prospered thanks to the rich coal fields and all the associated industries that went with coal mining. But the riches did not last, the coal supplies dwindled and as the pits became increasingly uneconomical to work and foreign imports became cheaper Whitley Bay, like so many of the its neighbours, began to go into decline. The arrival of the railway from Newcastle in 1882 proved a saviour for Whitley Bay and soon it had reinvented itself as a seaside resort. And it had much to recommend it, not least its long, sandy beach. Well into the twentieth century the resort provided thousands of holiday makers with happy memories every year. The promenade was developed, hotels and guest houses sprang up and The Links, a sea front park, was set out. The Links still host the occasional fairground but once, Whitley Bay had a permanent fairground: the Spanish City.

Hardly on the scale of Atlantic City, the Spanish City, an Edwardian pleasure palace boasting a spectacular dome, was opened in 1910 and was the site of a permanent fairground and amusement centre. It flourished for years, providing holiday makers through the decades with fond memories and somewhere indoors to shelter from the occasional English summer rains. Dire Straits wrote a song about it and as I cycled past I found myself humming and occasionally bursting into song with 'The Tunnel of Love' (much to the shock of the occasional dog walker). By the 1970s many Brits were holidaying abroad and just as the coal had run out so did the tourists. The Spanish City closed and, exposed to the merciless North Sea winter storms, the building began to decay. That could have been the sad ending of a lovely old building had it not been for some committed enthusiasts and a big chunk of funding. The Spanish City, I am pleased to say, has been saved and is now being regenerated. So if you're planning a hen or stag night, don't want the expense of going abroad but still fancy a bit of foreign culture and want to be able to brag you had a stag night at a Spanish City – might I suggest Whitley Bay?

The land around Whitley Bay first gets a mention in historical records around the early years of the twelfth century when it was granted to Tynemouth Priory. But land is power and in the years following the Norman Conquest there was much to-ing and fro-ing of land as men of powerful families fell in and out of favour with the ruling monarchs. Eventually the land was granted to Dudley, Earl of Warwick and Duke of Northumberland, a member of the influential Percy family. I was to come across more of them later.

Whitley Sands came to an end at a nature reserve and a headland. By this time I had left the promenade and was riding on a cycle path alongside a dual carriageway. I was still one of only a few people about, which did make me wonder of the necessity for a dual carriageway at that point. From the dual carriageway a cycle route led away past the nature reserve and across the headland overlooking a causeway to St Mary's Lighthouse.

Painted a dazzling white and perched on the little sandstone island, which is now itself a nature reserve, the lighthouse was built in 1898 and was in use for a little under one hundred years before being taken out of service in 1984. Long before the lighthouse and other buildings had occupied the rocky isle there had been a medieval chapel situated there; dedicated not, as you might expect, to St Mary but to St Helen.

Looking south I could see the curving line of Whitley Sands, the buildings of Whitley Bay hugging the low cliffs, the church tower picked out against the blue sky, and beyond the town much further to the south and jutting out into the North Sea was the lighthouse near Tynemouth. This relatively flat coastline made for easy, pleasant cycling, and the well sign posted route I was following made it virtually impossible to get lost, even for me. I reached Hartley and, in quick succession, Seaton Sluice along a pleasant traffic-free path running close to the coast. Short cropped grass, coloured with purple vetch and delicate yellow birds foot trefoil was attracting bumble bees and other insects that buzzed past me, sparrows called and flew amongst the occasional shrubs and gulls wheeled overhead. Out to sea an oil tanker sat on the horizon, its distant profile long and low. I cycled along to the noise of my wheels and the gentle sound of waves lapping the shore.

Salt had been the enduring mainstay of the economy on this part of the coastline for hundreds of years. Named after salt pans, Hartley Pans, as the area was known, had been making salt by traditional methods of evaporating brine since 1236. Taxation did for the industry as it has done for others, by the time of the Napoleonic Wars the increasing tax on salt resulted in the industry declining. Buying salt to sprinkle on your fish and chips was one thing but funding a foreign war through taxation quite another! As salt became prohibitively expensive this traditional, local industry virtually died out.

Half a mile to the north of the quiet village of Hartley is Seaton Sluice. I stood astride the bike, looking down into the little harbour to take a photograph of a few small pleasure craft and little fishing dinghies bobbing at anchor or moored to the deep stone walls of the harbour. It looked a peaceful haven on that bright sunny morning but in the middle of a winter storm the harbour would provide safe refuge against the pounding seas.

Seaton Sluice is a natural harbour but it gets its name thanks to improvements made on the inlet a few hundred years ago by local landowner Sir Ralph Delaval. The natural harbour was prone to silting up and so, under the direction of Sir Ralph, sluice gates were constructed. These gates used water trapped at high tide to flush out the silt at low tide. In the 1760s a channel was blasted through the rocks, the channel could be closed off at either end, thus solving forever the problem of loading at low tide. This tiny port played an important part in the trade of coal and glass in the region, keeping local families in employment and the local landowners, the Delavals, in the manner to which they were accustomed.

Key players in the area, the Delavals built the nearby Seaton Delaval Hall. The present Hall, a rather grand pile in the Baroque style, was built for Admiral George Delaval in the first half of the eighteenth century. But there had been settlements on the site since Norman times and a chapel from that era is still in existence today. It is not difficult to work out the family name has a bit of a French ring to it. The family were supporters of William the Conqueror, fighting alongside him at the Battle of Hastings. As a thank you for a job well done, good old Will granted them lands that, until King Harold had taken an arrow to the eyeball, had belonged to one of Harold's supporters. Such are the origins of many of the landed gentry of England! Not everything went well for the Delavals though! And in 1822 some dope left a candle burning next to a curtain, or a fell asleep whilst smoking in bed, or some other such careless thing, and the house caught fire. It took forty years to rectify the damage, (they had my sympathy: I had an insurance claim like that once, caused by a burst pipe though not a fire)!

Seaton Sluice is considerably different now to what it once was. The three hundred ton ships are gone, so too is the immense bottle works that once dominated the harbour side. Old photographs show the factory with its six large cones, like a child's primitive sandcastle, towering over the accompanying buildings. The last of its type in the country, the bottle works were started here in the eighteenth century by another Delaval, Sir Francis this time. The raw materials and fuel needed were in plentiful supply, and the natural harbour provided the ideal location from which to export the bottles and glass. By 1777 the factory was producing one and three quarter million bottles per year. (A modern parallel could, I thought, be drawn between that and the number of bottles consumed by the stags and hens of Whitley Bay)! No wonder the Delavals could afford such a large house! A village quickly grew to supply all the accompanying trades for the bottle works and for its employees, including a market place and the vital brewery which presumably sourced bottles for its beer very locally indeed.

When the nearby Hartley Pit closed it sounded the death knell for Seaton Sluice. By 1871 the bottle works too had closed, defeated by modern methods and overseas competition. By the turn of the century there was not a trace of the bottle works, it had all been demolished.

The tea from breakfast had long since been filtered from my blood stream and was pressing urgently on my bladder, so it was with relief in more ways than one that I spotted the public toilets just beyond Seaton Sluice and stopped to spend a penny. As a long distance walker and cyclist I've spent many a penny in a great variety of public toilets up and down the country. Some are nice and some are not and sometimes I've found myself wishing for a bush to hide behind rather than face the grimness and filth and biohazard condition of the public conveniences on offer. These were middle of the road, not too dirty, not too vandalised and not too dark to see what you were stepping in. The Goldilocks of public toilets are a rare thing. Ever since venturing into the ladies at Berry Head on the South West Coast Path I have looked warily for what might be lurking not so much on the seat as all around it. How anyone could miss the bowl quite so comprehensively as to cover the outside of it and even under the bowl is beyond me. That takes some doing, it must be a one off, I remember thinking as I hurried out of that particular cubicle without stopping to relieve myself. But it hadn't been a one off. I had walked innocently into les toilettes in a provincial market town in France some years later only to find the one and only cubicle in the same condition. "Merde!" I had muttered before hurrying out.

I have often contemplated the mentality of people who use public toilets for things other than going to the toilet. Not sure if that says more about me or them really! At the college where I work there is a shortage of staff toilets and rather than joining a queue I often use the student toilets which, by the end of the day, are beginning to get a bit grim. So why do some students when given a choice of a nice common room, picnic benches and a large canteen decide to eat their lunch sitting on the toilet surrounded by other cubicles, various unpleasant smells (including but not limited to pee, poo, fart, hairspray and perfume), and endure people rattling the door, flushing toilets, using the hand drier, etc. etc? How do I know they eat their lunch in the toilet cubicles? No, I don't make a habit of peering under the door or standing on the seat and looking into the neighbouring cubicle! I'd quickly find myself on a disciplinary if I did – child protection issues and all that! It's just that whenever I use the student toilets there is always a half-eaten sandwich, a can of pop or an empty chocolate wrapper or bag of crisps sitting on top of the sanitary bin! I wouldn't want to eat in my own toilet never mind any others.

So as I entered the public loos just north of Seaton Sluice I made sure to leave my supply of tea bags, chocolate and biscuits in the pannier. Although I did take my purse and mobile, well you can never be too careful. A sign inside asked users to respect the toilets and it reminded me of the ones in Staveley in Cumbria that I had popped into whilst cycling through there. Those particular toilets were cleaned by volunteers from the local community, a way of keeping them open I supposed during a time of public cut backs. They were clean and obviously the similar notice there asking users to make a donation (monetary, you understand) and respect the facilities was working: the Staveley toilets were clean enough for a student to eat their dinner off. But what struck me most was that they were twinned with some toilets in Cambodia! There was even a framed photo on the wall of the Cambodian toilet in question; it showed a simple concrete block structure with a doorway covered by a rough piece of sacking and it put into perspective how lucky we are and how much we take for granted in our modern public toilets. I bet that loo didn't have hot and cold running water, electric hand drier and tampon dispenser. Then again I bet no teenage girls ate their lunches in there.

A traffic-free cycle path hugged the coast, running through farmland and passing a few farm buildings before I reached the outskirts of Blyth. It was another level, easy couple of miles of cycling. Sheep and their nearly full grown lambs grazed the fields, watching inquisitively as I cycled past. I had moved on from 'Tunnel of Love' and was gradually working my way through the Sultans of Swing album, but my atonal rendition of 'Money for Nothing' was clearly doing nothing for the sheep. I never did get into the school choir, the teacher told my mother I was singing in the wrong key. My musical abilities stopped at the triangle and the recorder and even my recorder soon disappeared, although both my parents always denied all knowledge.

Blyth seemed smaller but grimmer than Whitley Bay. It too was yet another former prosperous port that had gone into decline. The River Blyth meets the coast at Blyth, flowing round a sharp bend between the town and a narrow spit of land to the north east providing protection to the mouth of the river. A long harbour wall constructed at the end of the spit provides further shelter and contributed to the success of the port during its heyday. Few ships use the harbour today and the east pier now has another purpose as home to a wind farm. Nine large turbines set in a line along the pier could easily been seen as I neared the town from the south. Wind farms are controversial with many people objecting to their appearance, claiming they spoil the landscape, but here particularly I thought they enhanced the view and they were certainly much nicer to look at than the grim power station situated on the north bank of the river a little further inland.

Perhaps if the cycle route had continued along the coast road I might have formed a better opinion of Blyth but it didn't. Instead, to avoid a busy main road, the cycle route wove about through the middle of town, challenging my map reading and navigational skills as it led me through a maze of side streets, over disused railway lines and across busy roundabouts where Saturday shoppers drove like dodgem cars to get into and out of the superstore, until finally I was disgorged onto a cycle path alongside another main road. Just when I thought it was all over the cycle route shot off to the left through another series of junctions and turnings at Bedlington Station. Congratulating myself on not getting lost I reached East Sleekburn and promptly got lost.

I am not quite sure how I missed the signpost directing me left, but I did. Maybe the sun was in my eyes, maybe my blood sugar was low (what, after all that breakfast?), maybe some little yob had moved the sign post, maybe I was distracted by a cloud of peacock butterflies that were flocking round the buddleia bushes or maybe I was too busy trying to remember the second verse of 'Twisting by the Pool'. Whatever my excuse, before I knew it I had cycled a mile in the wrong direction and had reached the ugly power station. Chain link fence, scrubby wasteland and concrete buildings marred the landscape, and the sound of the sea was obliterated by the hum of high tension power lines and the rumbling engine of a lorry idling at the kerb. I looked about me. I looked at my map. And then I looked a right idiot as, watched by the lorry driver drinking coffee in his cab, I turned my bike around and cycled back the way I had come.

The butterflies were still hovering around the buddleia bush and the signpost I had missed on the way out was clearly visible. I turned right, passed through East Sleekburn and over the dual carriageway without further incident and followed minor roads away towards West Sleekburn. But before I even got there a sign directed me back towards the dual carriageway and a cycle path running alongside it. Traffic roared up and down the tarmac, the sun beat down, exhaust fumes and dust blew into my face. Newbiggin-by-the-Sea passed distant and unattainable to the east. That was on the coast – why couldn't I cycle through it? I passed Ashington and North Seaton, still shadowing the dual carriageway.

Now with a dry throat and mouth, I was eager for a drink but determined not to stop until I had reached somewhere a bit more salubrious. I was just beginning to think the Coast and Castles should be renamed the Coast and Carriageway when a sign appeared directing me right into Queen Elizabeth II Jubilee Country Park. Yippee country! Well, yes, but only just. This was reclaimed ex-industrial land: we're not talking Wyoming here. I skirted a small lake with a few ducks and swans being thrown bread by young families, and I really should have stopped there for a mid-morning break but I was hankering after somewhere a bit more peaceful: more coast and less people. So I pressed on and soon found myself on another cycle track alongside a road, albeit not a dual carriageway this time, skirting an aluminium works to my left with yet another power station over to the right.

Both of these industries existed here because of coal mining in the area; the coal fuelled the factories and power stations of the industrial northeast. Tyne and

Wear was one of many regions throughout Britain with rich coal seams, and as the industrial revolution got into gear its demand for coal was unquenchable. Pits sprang up all around this area. The nearby Woodhorn Colliery Museum just to the east of Ashington gave an insightful and at times moving account of the history of the mines, the dangers faced by the miners and the hardships endured by whole communities of families whose livelihoods depended on coal.

Ashington and Woodhorn were sitting on a large coal deposit. The first shaft to be sunk was quickly followed by four more. At its height the colliery was producing a staggering 600,000 tonnes of coal each year and employing two thousand men. Men who, together with their families, needed housing. Rows and rows of cheap terraced housing were quickly erected, earning the community the nickname of 'the biggest village in the world'. And like so many of their compatriots during the great days of heavy industry, the miners toiled and were paid a pittance, enduring dangerous and sometimes deadly working conditions whilst the mine owners grew rich.

Eventually, following the Second World War, the Government privatised all the coal mines; the National Coal Board took over the running of all the coal mines in the country on the first day of the New Year in 1947. Safety, wages and working conditions improved. But the privatisation wasn't solely done on altruistic grounds; it had been apparent during both World Wars that the country needed a reliable, coordinated supply of coal. The mines had already been brought under Government control during the Second World War; Bevan boys being conscripted to go down the mines in the same way other men were conscripted to join the armed forces. It was a hard life, with tough working conditions and many dangers; accidents in the mine were common occurrences and deaths not infrequent, many Bevan boys often wished their contribution to the war effort had been fighting rather than mining.

The turbulent 1970s saw many strikes across various industries in Britain. Although only seven years old, I remember Edward Heath's introduction of the three day week in 1974, and the direct affect that had on my father at the time. Power cuts were common place, and many long winter evenings were spent reading by candlelight whilst the electricity supply was turned off. In 1972 and again in 1974 the National Union of Mineworkers went on strike, campaigning for better pay. They were victorious. The strikes, the union and the politics of the time divided opinion. Then in 1979, a former food scientist and grocer's daughter was elected the first female Prime Minister of the country. The unions had met their match. What Margaret Thatcher had formerly done for ice cream, that is ruined it, (cream-less ice cream consisting of an emulsion of water, skimmed milk powder, vegetable oils and sugar – come on, I ask you!) she now set about doing to British industry.

In 1980, as some pits became no longer viable, in part due to being worked out and in part due to competition from overseas, there were mass pit closures up and down the country. Some European governments, particularly France and Germany, were heavily subsidising their coal; meanwhile the cheaper method of open cast mining, taking place in various parts of the world, soon meant British coal was too expensive. In 1984, as unproductive and uneconomical pits continued to close, the N.U.M. called a national strike. This time the miners weren't fighting for money they were fighting for their livelihoods. And this time, they were not victorious. Mines closed, men lost their jobs, subsidiary industries were also affected and even more jobs were lost as a result. Communities died.

And when I watch the film Billy Elliot today, with the scenes with the rows of police and miners squaring off to one another, the desolation, the prize family piano being chopped up for fire wood, the mounted police charging the picketing miners, the sheer hopeless desperation felt by the characters involved, it reminds me what a miserable time the early 1980s was. Shortly after the film was released onto DVD, someone leant my mum and dad a copy.

"But mum," I said aghast, "you've not watched it have you? There's quite a bit of swearing in it!"

And my deeply religious mother, whose idea of swearing barely extended beyond 'hell fire', replied, "Yes I have. It was awful."

"Well I could have warned you about all the swearing!" I said.

"Oh, that didn't bother me," she exclaimed.

"But you just said it was awful!"

"Yes, what those poor miners put up with! Every night it was on the news, the police charging with batons, the soup kitchens and that bloody woman…"

I had no need to ask who she was referring to! By the 1994, when 'that bloody woman' had left office, there were just fifteen coal mines remaining in the country. And regardless of your political opinions, the loss of a once great industry can surely only be seen as a tragedy.

Soon after, just beyond Lynemouth, I finally left the industrial northeast behind for good. I was on a minor road cycling back to the coast at Snab Point and the start of the beautiful Druridge Bay. Nature Reserves and Country Parks followed one another in quick succession and I was spoilt for choice of locations for a lunch break. At Cresswell there was a little shop marked on my map and I called in to supplement my sandwiches (brought from home the previous day) with crisps and a fizzy drink. I cycled a little further to Cresswell Pond Nature Reserve and, leaning the bike on a nearby fence, stopped to have an early lunch.

My cheese and pickle sandwiches had survived the bouncing around in the panniers but my chocolate had suffered a bit during the sunny morning. I had started the day cycling in leggings and a light-weight fleece jumper, but as the temperature continued to rise that first day of June, those had quickly been removed to reveal my cycling shorts and short sleeved top, and as I sat in the full sun eating lunch I began to feel too hot even in those.

Packing up the wrappings from lunch and carefully stowing them in the panniers, I set off once more. The day was becoming increasingly hot but at least I had a gentle sea breeze to help keep me cool, and with no significant hills I shouldn't get too sweaty. I still had quite a distance to reach my B&B that night at Seahouses but checking my map I could see I had a scenic and interesting afternoon in prospect with lots of coastline, villages and my first two castles.

Full of food and anticipation I cycled on, along a rather rough track towards more ponds at Druridge Pools. This nature reserve was owned by Northumberland Wildlife Trust and until 1987 had been the site of an open cast coal mine. The nature reserve consisted of a collection of pools of varying sizes and a couple of marshy fields, and was an important site for numerous over-wintering migrants, as well as a breeding ground for many of our native wading birds and waterfowl. I stopped to see what I could spot, joining a small group of people watching a family of coots on the water and another family of moorhens feeding in the rushes. The moorhen chicks were just black balls of fluff with tiny bright red beaks, they timidly darted about between the tall stems. The coots on the other hand were much bolder, swimming confidently across the open water. An information board recorded recent sightings. I read down the list, yes I too had seen the skylarks and a meadow pipit. Someone had recorded seeing a hobby, one of our smallest birds of prey, hunting for dragonflies across the ponds. I didn't see one and I'm not entirely sure I would have recognised it if I had.

Back on the bike I hugged the coastline, passing more nature reserves and beautiful quiet seascapes until I reached Hauxley just to the south of Amble. Across a short stretch of sandy beach and a narrow channel of sea was Coquet Island. This egg shaped island, just a few hundred yards long, was yet another nature reserve, this time owned by the Royal Society for the Protection of Birds, and was an important breeding ground for over thirty-five thousand nesting birds. Imagine someone counting them all! And what if they got distracted (maybe by being poo-ed on) and lost count? Within those thousands of birds there is an important colony of the endangered roseate terns, whose protection has been ensured by providing nesting boxes to protect against predators such as gulls. Other species include arctic, sandwich and common terns, kittiwakes, fulmars, eider ducks and several species of gull, (some of which no doubt are now rather disappointed that roseate tern has been removed from the menu)! The birds I couldn't see from this distance, but the white lighthouse stood out brightly against the blue sea. The lighthouse, constructed in the 1841 at a cost of just over £3000, incorporates the remains of part of a medieval monastery. The first lighthouse keeper was one William Darling, brother of a young woman who was to make a bit of a name for herself.

The sun was positively beating down as I cycled along the coast and into 'the friendliest port', as Amble stiles itself.

"Hello," I greeted a lady cyclist as we rode past each other in opposite directions.

No reply. Not very friendly, I thought. Maybe she wasn't a local!

Friendly or otherwise, Amble is yet another small port that owed its livelihood in days gone by to the export of coal. Not anymore. It hasn't sunk to hosting raucous stag and hen parties; well not as far as I could tell – not a blonde wig or purple high heel in sight – but tourism of a more family-orientated nature, boosted by the annual Puffin Festival, is now the mainstay of the port. Holiday cottages and quaint guest houses lined the streets behind the modern marina, where expensive looking yachts bobbed against their moorings. A small fishing industry does still survive, providing fresh local catch for the fish and chip shops, cockle stalls and more upmarket restaurants in the area.

Cycling slowly along the smoothly surfaced streets, it was clear that much investment had gone into improving the little port and pulling in the tourists. I stopped at the tourist information centre near the sea front to buy a postcard, and was sorely tempted by the range of attractive puffin and lighthouse themed china cups and beakers on display. Should I buy one? And if I did would it make it home in one piece? I had a history of breaking cups just taking them out of the cupboard. Cycling with one for the next two hundred miles? The cup wouldn't stand a chance!

From Amble the cycle route diverted inland for a mile or so, sandwiched between a main road on one side and the River Coquet on the other. Despite the road it was a pleasant stretch, the river bank picturesque with wild flowers and the water full of ducks and a family of swans.

Following the river I reached Warkworth and the imposing castle. There has been a castle of some description on the site since the mid 1100s, but the first was thought too weak to defend against the Scottish invaders. It was later strengthened and added to at the onset of the Anglo / Scottish Wars, a conflict that came to shape the landscape I was cycling through.

The castle dominates the little town; its tower, well, er, towering, above the surrounding landscape; and the family most associated with the castle dominated English history. The Percy family produced Harry Hotspur, a knight and supporter of Henry Bolingbroke who, with the help of Hotspur in battle, was successful in his fight to be crowned King Henry IV. As a thank you for his support, Hotspur was granted lands in the region and continued to be a loyal subject until, after a big falling out with King Henry, he eventually revolted. But typical of medieval kings and nobles, they couldn't just stop sending Christmas cards or delete each other from their Facebook pages, instead they had to go and start a bit of a fight. Hotspur came off worst and was killed in battle, it is thought at Shrewsbury in 1403. Not content with the death of his former loyal subject and to refute claims that Harry was not really dead, King Henry had his body exhumed, chopped into quarters and beheaded and the parts sent around the country as a warning to others. And people talk about a woman scorned!

Warkworth Castle features in Shakespeare's Henry IV, described as 'this worm-eaten hold of ragged stone'. Well, I'm not sure about the worms, but the castle does have a slightly ragged appearance to it now some four hundred years after Shakespeare's less than flattering description. In parts, the walls of this Grade One listed building and Scheduled Ancient Monument are definitely ragged, whilst other areas of the castle are remarkably well preserved. The keep, the turrets, tower and many of the rooms remaining intact and giving a real feel for how things once were. I paid my money and wandered through the site, regretting I had so little time to fully appreciate everything. The Percy lion, the family emblem, is carved above the entrance to the Lion Tower, although over the centuries it has suffered from erosion. If you didn't know you would be hard pressed to correctly identify the animal it is supposed to represent.

Leaving the castle after all too short a time, I freewheeled down the hill into the village of Warkworth. Although the village has existed for centuries, most of the houses and shops lining the main street, with their mellow stones and red tile roofs, date from the eighteenth and nineteenth centuries. Near the bottom of the hill I reached the older market cross and the Norman church. I was tempted by a nearby café, displaying a mouth-watering assortment of cakes in the window, including my favourite dessert, lemon meringue pie. But the afternoon was getting on and I still had some distance to go. As I turned to cycle away a young man riding a recumbent appeared near the top of the hill and cycled swiftly down. Recumbents are supposed to be a very efficient way of cycling, but to me they always look very unstable and, with the rider quite low to the ground, must make it difficult to see and be seen. Not to mention the cyclist would be too low to see any lemon meringue pies sitting in café windows. No, a recumbent wouldn't do for me!

The next five miles followed minor roads weaving about through the countryside. Shortly after leaving Warkworth I passed Hermitage Farm, named after the hermitage that had existed near to the village during the fourteenth and fifteenth centuries. The hermitage had been established by the Percys, and was a cave hewn from the rock and consisting of a little chapel and several other chambers to house a priest. The priest was employed to pray for the souls of the family and their friends. Records show that the last hermit to live there in the 1530s received an annual stipend equivalent to £13.30 in today's money, and was also entitled to two loads of wood, a pasture for his beasts and 'a draught of fish every Sunday'. Living in a cave in the woods I bet it wasn't the only draught he experienced!

A gentle climb carried me to the highest hill thus far at around three hundred feet above sea level, and then it was a descent, quite steep at one point, heading east and back to the coast at Alnmouth. Alnmouth is tiny: a few cottages, a shop, a couple of places of worship, tea room and beach. I was through it before I had even realised, and was once more following minor roads waggling about, sometimes touching the coast and sometimes veering off inland, before returning to the coast again at Boulmer.

There is not a great deal at Boulmer. Just inland is R.A.F. Boulmer and in the village itself are a pub, some toilets, a church, a telephone box and, for me, a decision to make. The decision in question was whether to stick to the official route and continue to follow the minor roads which would once again carry me away from the coast, or stick to the coast along a track that was annotated on my map as an alternative route that was 'steep and rough in places'. It was a difficult decision, up there with tiffin or caramel shortbread. I wanted to stay on the coast but at the same time I was very much aware of the limitations of off-roading with my hybrid bike. If only I'd bought that puffin cup the decision would have been made for me! As it was I decided to play safe, and turned inland once more, past the R.A.F. base, through Longhoughton and along some beautiful wooded lanes before returning to the coast some four miles later at Howick.

A brief glimpse of sea and then I was off inland again. But the route was enjoyable and the scenery lovely, and the sea was never out of sight for long on the horizon to my right. I reached the lane leading down to the fishing village of Craster at around four o'clock. Craster I did not want to miss and so left the official route to cycle down to the tiny harbour, passing a tea room on the way where I stopped for a pot of tea and, coincidentally, a too delicious to miss piece of caramel shortbread. Feeling much refreshed and glad to have spent some time in the shade, I left the popular tea room, heaved my leg back over the bike and carried on down the lane.

Craster is famous for its smoked fish, kippers and salmon being a particular speciality of the family run Craster Smokehouse. (A fact I would have done well to remember as I reached the shoreline). The tide was coming in and I stopped to watch some birds bobbing in the waves about fifty yards or so off shore. Not much seemed to be happening in this sleepy little spot. Then suddenly an alarm went off! House? Car? Fire? Yes, fire! Looking round I spotted a small building tucked back from the shore with smoke pouring from it. What should I do? I could not imagine there was a fire station anywhere nearby. Suddenly from all directions people appeared and started dashing towards the harbour. From somewhere beyond the burning building a car roared into view, driving at lunatic speeds through the winding narrow streets. Was that the arsonist trying to escape? But he didn't look like he had planned his escape very well because he swerved to a halt near the harbour, leapt out and ran, as fast as he could in a pair of wellingtons, towards a building on the shore, the same building that all the other people, also in wellingtons, seemed to be sprinting towards.

"Julia," I said to myself, "you're an idiot!"

"Pardon?" gasped an elderly chap as he dashed past, clomping along in yet another pair of wellingtons. Oh, maybe I didn't say it to myself after all!

There was no fire. The alarm was coming from the lifeboat station. The arsonist wasn't an arsonist. And the blazing building was actually a smoke house! Within minutes a lifeboat was launched and powering out across the waves, scattering the sea birds and disappearing down the coast. Peace returned to the sleepy, fish-smoking village.

I turned left, following a track running in a straight line cutting across the back of the headland to the north on which Dunstanburgh Castle ruins were situated. The track was marked on my map as a proposed route but between the map being printed and me arriving at Craster the proposed route had obviously become a reality because all the cycle route signs pointed me in that direction. Something I was rather pleased about as I was to get spectacular views of the castle ruins.

Dunstanburgh Castle sits on a headland, a rocky outcrop to the south of Embleton Bay, and a strategically important position when the castle was first constructed in the fourteenth century. The largest castle in Northumbria, and one of the largest in northern England, it was built for Earl Thomas of Lancaster. Towards the end of the fourteenth century it was further strengthened and improved by John o'Gaunt, the Duke of Lancaster. And whilst the castle played little part in the border skirmishes with the Scots, it saw considerable action during the Wars of the Roses when it was held by Lancastrian forces. After a couple of sieges Dunstanburgh was left a little the worse for wear and the damage was never made good, it fell into a rapid decline, not helped as down the years the stones were recycled to use in other buildings. The imposing twin towers of the gatehouse consisted originally of four storeys, although little remains now of the third and fourth floors; and the once magnificent chambers with their grand fireplaces, designed to house the Earl's family, are now open to the sky.

Today the castle is owned by the National Trust, and looking towards it across the yellow fields of oil seed rape and the low gorse-covered outcrops, I could see that one part of the castle was undergoing restoration. A scaffolding tower climbed one turret; presumably crumbling masonry was being made stable. On such an exposed coast it seemed a miracle to me that the castle had survived so many centuries against the onslaught of winter storms and York sieges.

At Embleton, a village that had managed to retain its post office unlike so many others around the country, I found myself following a series of inland lanes once more. A couple of level crossings, an old airfield, a few gentle hills and a further nine miles and I reached the fishing port of Seahouses. I was booked into a Bed and Breakfast in the village and, stopping to take my accommodation list and directions out of my pannier, I set about finding the B&B. It didn't take much finding and I was soon being directed to leave my bike in the garage and ushered into a clean, tidy and homely house. The retired couple who owned it had relocated from the southeast and were living their dream in their long-loved Northumberland.

"We always said we would retire up here," explained the lady, as she insisted on taking my heavy panniers and proceeded to stagger upstairs with them. "This is your room here. You've a private bathroom just down the corridor, there's tea and coffee on a tray and if I've forgotten anything just give me a call."

"Thank you, this all looks lovely," I remarked, as I followed her into a bright, clean bedroom with a nautical theme.

"Now, I expect you're a bit peckish?"

"Well, I…" I began. But before I could explain I was still digesting a caramel shortbread and three cups of tea, she interrupted.

"I'll put the kettle on. I've just made a Victoria sandwich. Come down to the conservatory when you're ready."

"Thank you, I will."

So I did, and soon found myself being plied with large slices of cake and cups of tea. Fine by me! I had cycled sixty three miles, which is five miles farther than I was expecting to, according to the Sustrans map I should have travelled only fifty eight miles. But then, Sustrans couldn't be expected to make allowances for silly cyclists getting lost!

When the cake and the tea ran out I staggered back up to my room and began organising my luggage. I had a spare pair of underwear and socks and a clean top and some lightweight trousers for the evening. The cycling gear I had worn that day I intended to wash and leave to dry overnight. Taking my clothes and toiletries I popped down the corridor, locked myself in the bathroom and set about filling the large corner bath, adding a generous dollop of complimentary bubble bath (muscle-relaxing, according to the label – just what I needed).

Stripping off in front of the bathroom mirror, preparatory to hand washing my cycling gear, I got a bit of a shock. The sun must have been stronger than I had thought and my sun protection lotion not as protecting as I had anticipated. Everywhere not covered by my cycling shorts and top were turning a bright shade of boiled lobster! Freckles were sprouting out across my nose, and where my glasses had covered my face were two much paler circles, matched by the two white stripes where the straps of my cycle helmet had sat. In short, I was sunburnt. Not the best start to a cycling holiday, and I berated myself that I had not been more diligent with the sun lotion. I am blessed with the type of skin that browns quickly so I knew I wouldn't suffer too long but it was hardly a sensible thing to do, especially with the number of moles I have and warnings of protecting against skin cancer so often in the news.

With the cycling clothes washed, rinsed and wrung out, and the bath nearly full, I prepared to sink into a warm, muscling-relaxing bath. Should have tested the temperature first though!

"Julia, you moron!" I shrieked, as I plunged a foot and sunburnt ankle into the hot bath. "Bloody hell fire!"

"Everything all right dear?" came a concerned call from downstairs.

"Yes, thank you," I replied with deep embarrassment. "Water's a bit hot!"

How loudly had I shrieked? And had I sworn? I struggled to remember in the heat of the moment whether I'd cursed like a cross dresser on a stag night or merely sworn like a navvy. Letting some of the hot water out and running plenty of cold water into the bath, it was a few more minutes and some tentative testing before I finally deemed it safe to enter the muscle-relaxing bubble bath.

It was more than just my muscles that the bubble bath relaxed. I woke to find the water had gone cold and my fingers had gone all wrinkly. Swilling off under the shower, I quickly dried and dressed, gathered up my laundry and returned to the bedroom. Grabbing purse, mobile and laundry I went downstairs to find the owner and ask if I could use the washing line.

"Oh, you've caught the sun," remarked a fellow guest just tucking into tea and cake in the conservatory.

"Cycling," I said, as if that was all the explanation required. "Have you seen the owner?"

"I'm here," came a voice from behind me. "Oh, you've caught the sun."

"Yes," I agreed sheepishly, before asking about the washing line.

"I'll show you where it is," the lady replied and led me through the conservatory and out into the garden. "Are you off out for something to eat now?"

"Yes, I thought I'd have a walk down to the seafront and get some fish and chips." (Yes, okay, I know I'd just eaten loads of cake on top of other cake and sandwiches but it's hungry work cycling, and as my dad used to say, I have hollow legs)!

"You're welcome to bring them back and eat them in the dining room, but please don't take them up to your room," she said anxiously. "We had a couple here the other week and they brought a Chinese takeaway back and spilt it on the duvet."

"Don't worry, I won't do that," I assured her. "I was going to eat them sitting on the sea front."

"Oh, well in that case watch out for seagulls!" she laughed.

There are a disproportionate number of fish and chip shops in Seahouses. Far more than any other type of eatery, no surprise in a sea fishing port. Bamboozled by the choice on offer I did the only sensible thing and joined the longest queue outside a chippy that I could find. My rationale being that if people were prepared to queue for fifteen minutes for their meal then it must be good. By the time it was my turned to be served the smell was driving me mad and my growling stomach was earning me odd looks from others in the queue.

"Haddock and chips please," I said to the super morbidly obese walking advertisement for his own produce, when I reached the counter.

"Aye, you've caught the sun!" he commented in a warm northeast accent, grinning at my red and white striped face. "Anything else?"

"So I believe," I replied drily. "A carton of mushy peas please."

"Help yoursel' to salt and vinegar," he said, plonking a huge steaming portion of food on the counter top.

I do like a goodly amount of salt and vinegar on my fish and chips, it's the only time I add salt to my food and, grabbing the two condiments, I shook vigorously.

"Away lass, leave some for the rest of 'em," laughed the fryer, wrapping the fish and chips expertly in clean white paper and an outer casing of newspaper.

Exchanging what I thought was a ludicrously small amount of money for my fish supper, I hurried out of the shop and down to the seafront, finding an empty bench overlooking the shore. The seagulls left me alone, opting instead for an easier target in the form of two small children with ice creams, who wailed and screamed as one lost her flake and the other lost his entire ice cream. I watched the seabirds out on the waves, they appeared to be the same species as the ones I had seen earlier at Craster, but these were closer and I soon realised I was watching a flock of eider ducks. Eider as in down. These ducks had such soft feathers that they had been used in their thousands to provide the filling for eiderdowns for decades, until that is everyone started developing allergies and hypo allergenic fillings became de rigour. A matter I am sure the ducks were much relieved about! The males' plumage was a striking contrast of black and white, whilst the females were a uniform drab grey/brown, much better for camouflage. The fledglings, bobbing in the waves and sometimes nearly being swamped by larger waves, were endearing balls of grey fluff.

The evening was beginning to cool off as I made my way back to the B&B. The washing on the line was almost dry and I took it up to my bedroom, draping it over the radiator to air. The tea making tray contained amongst the tea and coffee a sachet of hot chocolate and I sat up in bed, writing my diary and carefully drinking the hot chocolate, ensuring it didn't go the same way as that Chinese meal I had been warned about!

Chapter Three

I woke the following morning worrying about my sun burn and determined to make sure I applied enough sun protection that day. As predicted, my red sunburn had turned brown, so I was now sporting a brown and white striped face and looked not dissimilar to a Murray mint. But that day my sun screen was to take the form of long leggings and a waterproof jacket: the weather had taken a turn for the worse. As I went downstairs to breakfast the sun was hidden behind gathering grey clouds and I wasn't to see it again until Scotland.

The breakfast was delicious, the tea and toast never ending. A bit like the rain that was tapping against the glass of the dining room window.

"Are you cycling?" asked one guest.

"Yes," I replied round a mouthful of toast and marmalade.

"What do you do when it rains?" asked another guest.

"Get wet," I sighed.

"It's supposed to brighten up later," comforted the first guest.

"That's only in the south dear," replied her husband.

"Where are you cycling?" his wife asked me.

"North, unfortunately," I replied with a smile.

"Ah!" said his wife, clearly having run out of words of comfort.

It was still raining, but lightly, when I left some time later. I set off into a light shower wearing my waterproof jacket and already feeling too hot. The slightest hill or head wind would only make it worse. I did, however, have a shorter day planned and was intending doing a little more sight-seeing than the previous day. Between Seahouses and Berwick-upon-Tweed – my destination that evening – was first Bamburgh Castle and then Holy Island, and my intention was to spend some time looking at both.

I left Seahouses expecting to be following a minor road a little way inland. But as with many of the Sustrans routes, between the printing of the map and my cycling, the route had been improved and amended. Cycle route signs directed me instead along a cycle lane following the coast road. It was flat easy going with good, if rather grey, views across the foreshore and the sea to the Farne Islands lying a few miles offshore. The Farne Islands, a small archipelago of about thirty little islands, are an internationally important breeding ground for sea birds. St Cuthbert had, for a time, made the islands his home – but more of him later! Eider ducks, often called cuddy ducks after St Cuthbert, breed on the Farnes, along with over thirty other species of seabirds, including puffins; and for tourists and wildlife watchers seeking the 'ah' factor there is a thriving colony of grey seals.

A few years previously, whilst holidaying in Northumberland, I had taken a rather rough boat trip across to the Farnes. The boat had been crowded with couples and families and avid bird watchers. When we left the jetty at Seahouses everything had been flat calm but by the time the little boat had chugged half way to the islands the sea had turned choppy, and it only got worse.

Up until that point my water borne experiences had consisted of a hired motor boat on Coniston Water with my dad. I knew my dad didn't have sea legs as I had watched him turn green when I steered the little motor launch across the choppy wake of a much larger boat. I had quite enjoyed both the sensation of bobbing about and the amazement that any human could go quite that shade. But as for my own sea legs, or lack thereof, it was not until that boat trip to the Farne Islands that I found out just how my poor dad had felt!

I watched the horizon, I watched the sky, I regretted having a full English breakfast and I thought I was just about keeping things together until an Oriental lady sitting facing me began to rummage in her capacious rucksack and then proceeded to hand out plastic carrier bags. Suddenly everyone wanted one, and once one person started it seemed to result in a tidal wave of seasickness. Those passengers sitting by the gunwales simply hung their heads over the side and heaved. Those in the middle of the boat snatched frantically at the proffered carriers. I looked at the orange Sainsbury's carrier that had been thrust into my hand and I remember thinking what an apt colour it was. But despite the sensation of my internal organs coming up to meet my head every time the boat fell into a trough of water, despite the acrid smell of diesel fumes from the engine, despite the miserable sound of retching coming from my fellow passengers, despite the salt spray (at least I hoped it was salt spray) hitting my face, despite my full English breakfast lying like an oil slick in my stomach, I miraculously managed to hold on to my eggs and bacon.

As the boat docked on the island and the skipper began helping his green customers off the boat, struggling to hide his amusement in the process, I gratefully returned my carrier bag to the Oriental passenger. She seemed reluctant to take it at first until I reassured her it was empty, but then she smiled, nodded and in broken English suggested I might like to keep it for the return journey.

"No, thanks, I won't be needing it. I'm swimming back!" I had replied, leaving her to wonder if she had understood me correctly.

Having been there, done that, got the carrier bag, I had no burning desire to return to the Farne Islands and was quite happy just to cycle past and admire from afar.

Bamburgh Castle sits on the edge of the mainland to the north of the Farne Islands, on a low bluff of dolerite rock, some one hundred and fifty feet above sea level, with sand dunes on its landward sides. Once the capital of the Kingdom of Northumberland it was one of the best preserved castles I was to come across. I approached it along the dunes. Marram, lyme and couch grass covered the sand hills by the shoreline and further inland the dunes were colonised with low scrubby bushes such as sea buckthorn and willow and adorned with colourful wild flowers including many large bright red poppies. A sea of red, their heads were bowing and swaying in the breeze. Although the rain had stopped, it was nevertheless too cold to spot any lizards sunning themselves on the patches of bare sand, but I did see several rabbits nibbling the course grasses and darting through the dunes. Banded snails, their humbug coloured spiralling shells looking not dissimilar to my stripy sunburnt face, clung to the stems of the grasses or slowly progressed across the sand, an unexpected inhabitant of this predominantly dry environment. Distinctive yellow and black caterpillars, of the red and black cinnabar moths, chomped their way through the dusky green foliage of ragwort; the poisons they absorbed from the ragwort and their vivid colouration acting as deterrents for any hungry birds. Skylarks sang overhead and closer to hand sparrows and dunnocks flitted between the bushes, carefully avoiding chomping down on any cinnabar caterpillars, if they had any sense. All that was missing was some sunshine.

The shoreline along this part of the Northumberland coast boasts some of the most spectacular sandy beaches in the country. Not the obvious choice for a sunny English seaside holiday, these northeast beaches remain relatively quiet. With miles of clean golden sand, more than its fair share of historic castles and fabulous nature reserves the region is a remarkably unspoilt and little known holiday destination. And all the better for that in my opinion. There is nothing worse on a walking or cycling holiday to suddenly have your solitude and peace spoiled when you turn a corner or come round a headland and find you have arrived in a tourist hotspot, where holiday-makers abound, litter is everywhere except in the bins, and commercialism dominates. I don't mind the odd tea room, a little cluster of B&Bs or the village pub; but when you are suddenly faced with amusement arcades, souvenir shops, national pub chains and beaches crowded with folk, I just want to run screaming for the hills. Which probably explains why I always choose quiet places for activity based holidays, rather than spend two weeks every summer clubbing in a Spanish resort where I can get English food and Irish beer every ten yards.

So in short, Northumberland kind of appealed to me. Although at that point, cold and a little bit damp, I wouldn't have minded the kind of weather they get in Spain! I know: I'm never satisfied.

Although I had not gone far that morning, I felt a refreshment stop was in order and, leaving the bike secured to a fence, I took my drink and walked out onto the beach. There seemed to be a sand castle competition in progress, and whilst I am sure it had been intended for children there were more than a few competitive fathers getting involved.

"Shore that side up," directed one father to his young daughter.

"Sea shore, she shore, she shells," chanted his daughter, far too wrapped up in her own diggings to take any notice of dad.

"Never mind, I'll do it!" he sighed impatiently. "Here, put these flags on top this tower."

"She shells she sells on the see saw… Baa baa back sheet."

"Never mind, I'll do it!" he sighed again.

A few yards away an extended family were hard at work, with three generations of males all digging, mixing and building with wrapt concentration. Did the builder's van I had noticed parked on the road nearby belong to them? Father was stripped to the waist despite the less than warm June weather, and showing rather too much of a rather off-putting bit of bum cleavage. Grandfather had his shirt sleeves rolled up and seemed to be directing operations. Whilst identical twin boys were studiously ignoring both dad and granddad, furiously digging a channel stretching from the moat of their impressive castle in the direction of the distant sea.

"You've got too much water in your mixture," granddad suddenly snapped as a wing of the grand castle started to subside. "What am I always telling ya?"

"Sorry da," his son ruefully relied, hitching his trousers up and leaning back on his spade which promptly snapped, designed as it was for an eight year old. "Ah bugger!" he exclaimed as he fell flat on his back.

"Do that turret again, with a bit more sand this time lad."

"Aye, aw reet, da. Do you think anyone'll notice if I sneak in a bit of cement, like?"

Fearing I might burst out laughing if I sat too near, I took my drink and wandered a little further down the beach. A young boy, who seemed to be on his own, was standing back to admire something that seemed to have more flags, feathers and shells than sand. He looked up and saw me admiring it.

"What do you think? Will I win?" he asked me guilelessly.

"You might," I stammered, unsure what to say. "It's a very nice castle."

"Oh, it's not a castle," he replied.

"Oh, okay, what is it?"

"It's a brothel."

"! Er, do you mean a bothy?" I asked.

"What's one of them?"

"It's, well, it's a bit like a barn. But animals live in the bottom half and the farmer and his family live in the top half."

He regarded me quizzically for a few seconds. "Na, it's definitely a brothel."

"Not a castle?" I persisted, somewhat shocked.

"Na, a brothel. Where the soldiers visit."

"Soldiers live in castles."

"Yeah," he thought for a minute, before replying patiently, "but they visit a brothel. To see the Protestants."

I could think of nothing to say to that, other than, "oh, right. How old are you?"

"Nine."

Nine! I didn't even know what a brothel or a Protestant was at nine. And I went to a Church of England primary school!

I left the next Mr Stringfellow to his castle, brothel, house of ill repute or whatever it was, finished my drink and returned to the bike. A seagull had very kindly crapped on the saddle while I had been gone. I had a bit of a rant, cleaned the saddle with some tissues, put the tissues in a nearby litter bin, climbed on the bike and realised the saddle wasn't the only thing the gull had crapped on. I got off the bike, had a bit more of a rant, shook my fist at a passing herring gull and carefully removed my cycling gloves which were now black and white. More tissues, more cleaning of bike (handlebars this time), some ineffective cleaning of gloves, some more ranting. I was beginning to sound like a cross dresser on a stag night!

I left the bike and stomped off to the nearby toilets where, thankfully, there was plenty of soap and water. I must admit I got a few strange looks as I stood at the sink washing my hands with my gloves on, but it seemed the easiest way of washing them. I got some even stranger looks when I started to dry them. It was only as I came out of the toilets that I noticed the dye had run in the gloves. My cycling gloves were the fingerless type, and the ends of my fingers were now dark grey. Returning to the toilets I removed the gloves and washed my hands. They stayed dark grey. How can dye come out of gloves with the application of soap and water, but application of the same soap and water won't remove the same dye from skin? How does that work?

I half expected my bike to be covered in more gull guano but it was mercifully unsullied when I got back to it. I swung my bum onto the saddle and cycled off. Well, I say cycled off, and that was certainly my intention. However, in all the fun of crap removal I had forgotten that my bike was still chained to the fence. So I cycled all of two feet before the chain reached its limit. The bike stopped but I carried on going, and I was catapulted sideways off the bike. As I lay in a crumpled, swearing heap on the ground, I remembered this was not the first time a security chain and two wheels had got the better of me.

A few years earlier I had owned a moped. Well, actually I had owned two, the first one having been stolen and dumped into the Leeds and Liverpool Canal. So with the second moped I had become very security conscious and invested in a large, heavy duty chain. I had finished work one evening and gone out to where I had left the moped chained up in the car park. Unlocking the chain, I then opened the pannier, removed my helmet from said pannier and put it on my head, filling the now empty pannier with my bag. At which point my brain, after eight challenging hours at work, must have switched off. I climbed on the moped, put the key in the ignition, started the 49cc engine and set off. There was a colossal crunching and grinding noise from the rear end (the moped's - not mine) and the moped came to an immediate halt, which I remember thinking, was a first, as the brakes were usually dreadful. As with my bike, the moped stopped and I carried on going. And as with the bike, I found myself face down on the ground. That time at least I had got as far as unlocking the chain. But that was as far as I had got, for I had forgotten to take it off and put it in the pannier! The result I saw, once I picked myself and the moped up off the ground, was that the chain had whipped itself around the wheel as soon as I had attempted to ride away. Worse than that, the chain was well and truly lodged between the wheel and the wheel arch. Bracing my foot against the moped, I heaved and tugged (and yes, I guess I probably swore a bit too!) until finally I freed the chain. Riding home there were some mighty strange noises coming from the rear wheel. The moped spent quite a while afterwards in the garage and, consequently, I spent quite a bit of money in there!

I am a firm believer in learning from your mistakes. Pity I didn't learn from that one with the moped! Security chain duly removed from my bicycle, road grit picked out of my knees and nose, I got back on the bike and hurried off, hoping no one had seen my embarrassing escapade.

I left the Sustrans route, heading for the castle entrance, stunned as I drew nearer by just how large Bamburgh Castle is. As with Warkworth Castle, there has been a castle of some description on the site for close to a thousand years; the original one being little more than a wooden palisade. Sadly I did not have time to really do the castle full justice. It was the sort of place where I could easily have spent most of the day, but I could only spare a couple of hours.

There is more to Bamburgh than just its castle, although not much more. There's a church, a tea room and shop and the Grace Darling Museum. If I admired the brave men in their wellies charging off in their modern lifeboat to rescue someone in distress at Craster, how much more did I admire local heroine Grace Darling.

Born in 1815, at one of the little cottages in Bamburgh, she spent most of her life living in the lighthouses on the Farne Islands where her father, William, was lighthouse keeper. During a severe storm on a night in September 1838, Grace spotted a ship had been wrecked on Harcar Rocks about a mile from the island where the lighthouse stood. The Forfarshire, a paddle steamer, had floundered on the rocks and broken in two, the stern had sunk and some of the passengers and crew had somehow managed to cling on to the remaining half of the vessel. Together with her father, Grace watched as dawn finally provided enough light for them to see a small group of survivors huddled on the rocks. Fishermen watching from the shore had already judged the sea too dangerous to attempt a rescue and, from his lighthouse, Grace's father clearly thought the same. However, Grace had other ideas and persuaded her father to attempt a rescue.

Taking the small coble boat, Grace and her father rowed across the stormy sea to rescue the survivors. There were nine in all, forty-three passengers and crew already having drowned, and the coble was too small to take all the survivors at once. With Grace keeping the coble stable, William assisted some of the people onto the little boat and they rowed back to the lighthouse before making a perilous second trip back to the rock to rescue the remaining survivors.

Grace was hailed a national heroine, and both she and William were awarded the Gold Medal by the National Humane Society. But Grace had grown up in a sheltered community and the sudden and intrusive worldwide fame that the rescue had generated was more than she could cope with. National and even international newspapers ran the story, lauding her bravery. The status of 'celebrity' hardly existed then but that is what Grace suddenly became. She had poems, songs and plays written about her. She was invited to speak at different events, and was hounded by various groups, dignitaries and even members of the church. She received letters, money and even a proposal of marriage! Her portrait was painted. Souvenirs of her and her rescue were produced in great number: everything from cups, postcards, model boats and plastic action figures – okay they might have been cheap pottery figures, but even so!

Grace found the unwanted attention too much to bear. She refused to leave the lighthouse, a place of safety where she had spent most of her life. The fervour of interest was beyond anything she had anticipated and it marred her remaining life. On a rare journey to visit family, first on Coquet Island and then to Alnwick, she contracted tuberculosis. She died in her father's arm at the cottage in Bamburgh in 1842, aged just twenty-six.

From Bamburgh the cycle route took me inland. 'Take care crossing very busy road' said my map. It also said 'Vorsicht beim Uberqueren! Sehr stark befahrene Strasse'. Which translates from the German as 'take care crossing very busy road'. Why did my map have a warning in German? Well, this cycle route, together with others in the east of England and Scotland was part of the North Sea Cycle Route, a European cycle route that ran all around the North Sea through France, Belgium, Holland, Germany and across the Baltic into Scandinavia. A friend of mine had already done part of the route running along the Dutch coast and had highly recommended it; although I suspected part of his enthusiasm came from the fact it was flat and part from his memories of a topless bar he had found in Amsterdam. Flat cycling I wasn't averse to but topless bars didn't really do it for me.

The road that had elicited the warning from Sustrans was the A1 trunk road, a behemoth of a road that runs the length of the country and carries huge volumes of traffic every day. I approached it with caution, expecting a lengthy wait, and so was pleasantly surprised to find not a vehicle in sight and that I was able to cross it with ease.

Across the A1 I was faced with a steep climb into the village of Belford that left me sweating and cursing inside my waterproof. In fact I was sweating so much that I was wetter with my jacket on than off, so I decided to stop and remove it. With the jacket off I certainly felt a lot cooler and as the rain was no more than a light shower I continued for the next few miles in just my cycling T-shirt.

The countryside around me was a pleasant mixture of farmland and woodland, a scenic rolling landscape of varying shades of green. Ahead of me on the quiet lane a mouse scampered across the road unaware of my silent approach. A little further on and I was thrilled to watch a weasel dart out from the hedgerow and begin running down the lane towards me. Before I reached him he turned and disappeared into the neighbouring field.

Fenwick Wood came and went on my right and I began concentrating, keen not to miss a road on the right that would take me on a diversion to Holy Island. Holy Island, or Lindisfarne as it is also known, was not on the cycle route but I was eager to revisit this wonderful little island that I had last visited as a child with my parents. My mum had been particularly taken with it: possibly it had been the history that had so captivated her, or possibly the religious importance, or possibly the castle, or then again it could have been the crab sandwich she had for lunch there.

But before I could reach the island I had a few obstacles to negotiate. The first was the A1 again; it might have been quiet the first time I crossed but that certainly wasn't the case the second time. Cars, coaches, caravans and juggernauts raced past me as I stood at the side of the road, becoming increasingly impatient as the minutes ticked away and no safe gap appeared in the streaming lines of traffic. Eventually with my bike in my hands and my heart in my mouth I dashed across.

My next challenge was the East Coast Main Line, one of the busiest railway lines in the country and one of the fastest. Originally there were three companies operating the railway line from London to Aberdeen, a total of 393 miles; with this stretch of the line, running south from Berwick-upon-Tweed, owned and operated by the North East Railway Company. But that was back in the glory days. Eventually these three had merged. Then the railways were nationalised. And then they were privatised; and now this line is run by Rail Track, or rather the rails and all the twiddly bits are. The trains and services are run by Virgin, or it might be First ScotRail, or it might be East Coast, or Arriva, or Northern Rail, or Cross Country Trains, or First Great Western, or National Express East Anglia for all I know! Well I can't remember, there are now so many different companies operating so many services that just keeping up is a nightmare, and as for trying to buy a ticket for a journey that spans several operators, plus take a bike with you! Don't get me started! Pity it's not run by Deutsche Bahn or the Swiss railways – you could take any number of bikes on efficient, punctual trains if that were the case.

A sign warned people of the dangers of attempting to cross the line when the barriers were down. Surely no one would be daft enough to try? But the barriers were up, there was no train due and I cycled carefully, if bumpily, over the rails and down the hill towards the coast.

The final obstacle was the tidal causeway to Lindisfarne. And this really was pot luck as to whether I would be able to visit the island or not. At high tide and for some time either side of high tide, the causeway was impassable. If the tide was in I would not be able to cycle across – obviously! But if the tide was due in in the next few hours I would still not be able to cycle across as I would not have time to get back. As it turned out, tide times posted at the start of the causeway worked out well for me and I had plenty of time to cycle over to the island, look round, have lunch and cycle safely back to the mainland. The last thing I wanted was to get stranded on the island, as that would wreck my whole schedule.

As I set off across the long causeway the weather took a turn for the worse. A northerly wind picked up and the clouds descended and released copious quantities of rain. Half way along the causeway is a refuge, and I took refuge just long enough to put my waterproof jacket back on, dry my spectacles and blow my nose. Then it was back out onto the causeway, battling the sideways wind and rain, the salt spray, the condensation building up on the inside of my lenses and the rain on the outside. I bounced and skidded over the rutted tarmac, trying to dodge the seawater-filled pot holes and the slippery kelp, whilst at the same time trying not to avoid a pot hole at the risk of swerving into a passing car, of which there seemed to be a sudden continuous line. It was with a huge sigh of relief that I reached the island and gained a bit of shelter behind the dunes. The shelter was short lived as the wind suddenly changed direction, and started coming at me from the southwest carrying with it more seawater and a good quantity of sand. By the time I reached the more sheltered village I was soaking, salty and sandblasted, and the bike chain was making a nasty grinding noise with every revolution of the pedals.

A snack van was set up near the path leading down to the priory. I propped the bike on its stand and, fumbling with numb fingers for my purse, went to stand under the awning of the van and warm my hands on a much needed mug of tea. I had timed it just right, for as I stood under the awning, stamping my wet feet to keep warm, a sudden heavy shower launched a torrent of rain across the island. The view disappeared and the rain set up a relentless drumming on the roof of the van. The awning quickly built up a sagging pool of rainwater which I eyed warily, inching ever closer to the middle of the awning in the hope that when it either collapsed under the weight of water or drained off the edges, I would not be standing under the deluge.

A family were hurrying down the track to the van, desperately trying to keep dry under a single umbrella. Making a mad run for it, dad and the elder girl reached the shelter of the awning first. But mum and the younger girl were slower and very unlucky. Just as they were stepping under the awning a sudden gust of wind whipped the sagging canvas, it lifted and tipped its reservoir of rainwater down on their heads. The umbrella was swept to one side by the cascade of cold water, leaving the hapless pair standing drenched and dripping. The mum let out a shriek, the little girl began to cry but the dad and the other child let out roars of laughter which only served to make the mum even angrier. The guy behind the counter turned away and I could see his shoulders shaking as he tried to stifle his laughter. I too was struggling not to spill my tea.

"Never mind, love," said the dad between sniggers, a little too late, I thought, to save his marriage. "I'll buy you a cuppa."

His wife's only response was to whack him with the soggy umbrella. Violence obviously ran in the family, as the very wet younger child promptly launched an attack on her sibling, thumping ineffectually at the girl who continued to screech with laughter.

The rain soon stopped and a watery sun tried to make an appearance over the sea; it wasn't to last long but at least it tried long enough for me to explore the island. Lindisfarne is peaceful now but that has not always been the case. As I explored the tiny village with its rows of cottages, little squares and narrow streets, I was constantly reminded of island's dramatic past both in the names of the cottages and the abundant history all around me.

Down by the natural harbour just a few small fishing boats remain, the last of a fleet still making a living catching mainly lobster and crab, for which the island is justly famed. Outside several of the sturdy stone built cottages there were signs advertising crab sandwiches for sale. Some of the old fishing boats still survive, no longer seaworthy – anything but in fact – they have been sawn in half amidships, turned on end and are now used as sheds; different, I thought, but appealing nevertheless.

The island itself is designated as a nature reserve and is a Site of Special Scientific Interest. The waters around its shores are not just home to crabs and lobsters but a rich range of flora and fauna. The dunes themselves have a high biodiversity with many arctic species of plants; whilst the rocky shoreline, tidal marshes and mud flats all provide a diverse habitat for numerous birds. In winter, migrants arrive from the Arctic; and in spring and again in autumn thousands of migrating birds use Lindisfarne as a stopover on their migrations, fuelling up on the variety of plants and invertebrates that live in the mudflats and on the island.

Lindisfarne has been inhabited by man for millennia but it was a quiet chap called Aidan, a monk from Iona, who first put the island on the map. Invited by Oswald, King of Northumberland, in A.D. 635 Aidan and fellow monks arrived on the island with the purpose of founding a monastery. The first monastery was a simple wooden structure, of which nothing survives. Lindisfarne was a centre of missionary work throughout the north of England. After Aidan's death some fifteen years or so later, his worked continued under the direction of Cuthbert (he of the cuddy duck). Cuthbert was purported to have healing powers and eventually both he and Aidan were canonised posthumously. To celebrate Cuthbert becoming a saint, another Lindisfarne monk, Eadfrith, set about creating a series of illuminated manuscripts. These were to become known as the Lindisfarne Gospels, and amazingly despite all the turmoil that was to follow down the centuries, all that the monks of Lindisfarne endured, the Gospels still survive to this day. Richly illustrated with intricate script work and dazzling colours, the originals are now safely stored in the British Library, but copies are kept on Lindisfarne.

But while the monks were busy illustrating and praying and spreading the gospel, trouble was brewing on the horizon. The Vikings were coming. And they weren't just dropping by for a crab sandwich! In A.D. 793 they landed on Lindisfarne and set about raping, pillaging and generally spoiling everything they could lay their hands on. The Priory was destroyed, along with many of the monks, the lucky ones escaping to Durham with Cuthbert's remains and the Gospels. But that wasn't to be the only raid. The Vikings just kept on coming, and going, and then coming again, and then going. Raid after raid down the years, until eventually some of the Vikings went home whilst others stayed. And who can blame them? After all Briton was forever being invaded down the centuries: Romans, Angles, Saxons, Jutes, Vikings, Normans, French Huguenots, former colonials, Eastern Europeans: get over it! We're a real mongrel breed! Many of the place names in the north of England have Viking and Danish origins, and no doubt many of the people do too!

Fast forward a couple of hundred years and the monks returned to Lindisfarne, building another priory, a Benedictine one this time, in the eleventh century. This priory suffered considerably during the Border Wars with the Scots but its ultimate destruction came at the time of the Reformation during the reign of Henry VIII. However, it was not completely destroyed and its impressive ruins remain, including the striking Rainbow Arch, which forms a fragile looking curve between two columns, amongst the crumbling walls.

Another ecclesiastic building in better shape is the parish church. Still in use today, some parts of the walls and stonework, containing Saxon architecture, predate the Norman Conquest. And Holy Island itself remains a place of pilgrimage to this day.

The stones from the ruined priory were recycled, or up-cycled to use the current jargon. Many of them being used in the construction of Lindisfarne Castle. Built in 1550 to defend against the Scots, the castle sits in a good defensive position on Beblowe Crag, an outcrop of igneous rock, on the southeast corner of the island. It barely saw any action and in the early years of the twentieth century architect, Sir Edward Lutyens, started work to transform it into an Edwardian country house. Today it is owned by the National Trust and is a truly amazing place. I had already visited it when on Lindisfarne years ago with my parents and so had no intention of paying a repeat visit but I clearly remember the stunning interiors.

I spent at least an hour wandering this peaceful island, taking photographs, reading the information boards and watching the bird life, their calls a constant and relaxing background melody to my meanderings. The weather held off long enough for me to enjoy my time on Lindisfarne and to enjoy reminiscing about the time I had spent there with my mum and late father. I returned to the tea van for another cup of tea and an indulgent crab sandwich, and then bought a postcard to send to mum.

The clouds were closing in again and it was time to get back on my bike. The traffic seemed a bit lighter as I slipped and slid back across the causeway. It wasn't my imagination; the sea was considerably closer to the road as I headed back to the mainland. Thankfully the wind had eased, although the rain had begun again, a light drizzle that persisted for much of the remainder of the day.

Safely across the causeway and safely across the East Coast Main Line (still no sign of any trains) I crossed the busy A1 again. Then I puffed and heaved my way uphill to rejoin the official cycle route. Providing I didn't get lost, I calculated I had about twelve more miles to go that day. Twelve miles doesn't sound a lot but it was quite enough thank you. I was damp, my hands were cold, fingers going numb and my knees were aching.

The map informed me I was following a temporary route; plans were in place to make a more direct approach into Berwick along the coastline. I was a couple of years too early to enjoy what would surely be a nicer route. Instead I was back on minor roads, alternately wiping the rain off my handle bar-mounted map case and the rain and condensation off my face-mounted glasses, as I concentrated on seeing where I was going and not getting lost. The odd car passed me, spraying water over my feet. The even odder tractor also passed me, spraying water and other smelly things I did not want to contemplate over the rest of me. When, after the second soaking courtesy of Massey Ferguson, a large tractor towing a muck spreader came into view around the bend in front of me I hastily turned off down a convenient side lane and hid behind the hedge until the smelly threat had passed. Turning up to the B&B wet, cold and smelling a bit like a damp carpet was one thing, turning up covered in moisture and manure and smelling like a farm yard was something else. I was hardly likely to be invited into the sitting room for tea and cake if I arrived with the lingering scent of manure!

At some point on that journey there was another crossing of the railway. So far I had not seen any trains but that was about to change. I reached the sturdy fence guarding the railway and, next to it, a large information board. As I was about to begin reading the notices there was a loud whistle from behind me and a train thundered past at an earth-shuddering, ear-splitting, hair-parting rate. The ground, my feet, my bike and my teeth all vibrated. I was standing right by the fence and within touching distance of the hurtling intercity on the other side of the barrier. It felt like my world was being put through a blender. Carriage after carriage hurtled past in a blur of black and red livery. And then it was gone, a spec in the distance, leaving me swaying in the slipstream and inhaling the cloud of dust. Silence descended. Had I gone deaf? Then I sneezed. No, not deaf.

Turning my attention back to the notice board, which was now swaying gently, with its list of safety information, warnings and commands, I began to read the list of instructions and all the does and don'ts.

Obvious safety information, along the lines of: 'if a train is approaching do NOT cross the railway line'. Thanks, I'd never have worked that out for myself.

Prohibitions, such as: 'do NOT throw anything onto the railway line'. People actually had to be told that? Presumably yes!

Advice, such as: 'do NOT cross if you do not have time to reach the other side'. Well, duh!

Warnings, such as: 'danger of DEATH'. Yes, death was in capitals, as if to leave it in lower case would diminish the seriousness of death.

Vetoes, such as: 'do not tie damsels in distress to the railway lines'. Okay, I made that last one up. But there were so many instructions I would not have been surprised to have found one like it.

The list was long and mainly stated the obvious. If people needed telling not to leave a leaf on the line or the wrong type of snowman tied to the track or to stall their car in the middle of the rails and stay in it whilst a train was approaching maybe, I thought, they deserved to be taken out of the gene pool!

Of more relevance to me was the list of how to cross the line. I know, you're thinking I should perhaps be taken out of the gene pool too if I need to be told that, but! Humour me! It was all about the safest way of opening the gates. And this was something I needed to concentrate on, because these instructions were purposely aimed at the cyclist. And there was a long list of them!

1.   Always dismount and push your bicycle across. Do NOT attempt to ride your bicycle across the level crossing.

2.   Ensure there are no trains visible in either direction.

3.   Leave your bike at this side of the level crossing. Open the gate and walk across the tracks to the opposite gate.

4.   Open the opposite gate and secure it in the open position with the chain.

5.   Ensure there are no trains visible in either direction.

6.   Walk across the tracks to the first gate.

7.   Open the first gate and secure it in the open position with the chain.

8.   Ensure there are no trains visible in either direction.

9.   Collect your bicycle and wheel it across the level crossing. Walk. DO NOT RUN.

10.   Leave your bike in the bike stand beyond the gate.

11.   Ensure there are no trains visible in either direction.

12.   Walk across the tracks to the first gate.

13.   Close the first gate, ensuring it is securely latched.

14.   Ensure there are no trains visible in either direction.

15.   Walk across the tracks to the second gate.

16.   Close the second gate, ensuring it is securely latched.

I read the list of instructions, then I read them again just to make sure I knew what was expected of me. Then I realised I had forgotten point 4, so read them again. Then I decided to put them into action. Then there was an eardrum rendering whistle, the earth shook and the 14.15 from Kingscross roared past. It disappeared and peace descended. Now, where was I? I though it prudent to read the instructions again. Then I was ready.

Check for trains: check, all clear. Oops! Forgot to dismount. Dismount: check. Check for trains: check, all clear. Open gate. Check for trains, yes, still all clear. Walk calmly, safely and maturely across. (Maturely nothing to do with sensible and all to do with aged knees). Reach opposite gate, in one piece: check. Open gate and fasten back: check. Check for trains: check. Bloody hell, not another one! Cue earth shattering, ear piercing, dust disturbing, roaring intercity: the 15.20 from Aberdeen I presume? Where the hell had that come from? Yes, yes, I know: Aberdeen! But it hadn't been in sight five seconds previously.

Okay, so where was I? Check for trains: check, nothing in sight. (Surely there could be no more for a little while)? Walk across to first gate. Open first gate and secure in open position: check. Grab bike, underestimate weight of panniers and nearly topple it over. Check for trains: check, nothing coming. Wheel bicycle sedately over the railway line. Shove bike in stand on far side of second gate. Check for tra…. Another screeching whistle, thundering wheels, blurred carriages as the next train from points south hurtled north.

"My giddy aunt Fanny!" I squealed in fright, jumping in the air and nearly out of my skin. "How many more bloody trains? I'm not going to cross! There's no need to keep whistling at me! I'm more likely to have a bloody coronary than be hit by a bloody train at this rate! I bet there're not as many sodding trains when I'm at Edinburgh station waiting to come back!" I continued to rant.

A cow mooed in sympathy from a neighbouring field.

"Yes, I bet you're fed up of all this whistling, earth shaking shenanigans!" I sympathised.

"Well, you kind of get used to it when you live nearby," replied the cow.

"Eh?!"

Now I was hallucinating! Was it all that pressurised air blasting my eardrums? No. It was a woman I had not previously seen, walking towards me accompanied by a poodle on a retractable lead.

"Er, hmm, yes," I stuttered, deeply embarrassed, had she heard my outburst? "I suppose you do."

"It's okay, I'll close the far gate for you. I'm walking across," she added. Her dog rolled its bulging eyes, giving me a mad stare as she passed. Was the dog mad, or did it think I was?

"Oh, thanks. Much appreciated," I replied sheepishly, and, wrangling my bike out of the stand, I hurriedly mounted and cycled away.

The route marked on my map was, on the ground, little more than a field full of grass and sheep: a bridleway, fine if you were on horseback but not so good on two wheels. I cycled bumpily along, dropping into dips concealed by the long vegetation, the blades of grass making a strange shushing sound against the wheels. But for all that, this section of the route was very enjoyable. The narrow bridleway close to the edge of the cliffs was so completely different from anything else on the entire route that it was to become a highlight of my journey. The grey sky was all above me and to the right was the grey North Sea stretching to a horizon I could not distinguish. A few gulls floated on the wind, riding the thermals rising up above the low cliffs, their cries harsh and eerie in the darkening, wet afternoon. The tide was coming in; little remained of the sandy beach below me, just a narrowing strip of sand and some low, jagged rocks running in a series of parallel lines out into the waves.

A little further along and Berwick-upon-Tweed slowly hove into view to the north as I joined a better track sandwiched between the sea and the railway line. Then suddenly, it was downhill into Berwick, leaving the railway before it crossed the valley of the River Tweed on an impressive viaduct that looped clockwise through the town.

I had only cycled 30 miles that day, a relatively short distance and thankfully so considering the unseasonal cold, wet weather. Nowhere looks particularly nice in the rain and Berwick on that damp, prematurely dark early evening in June was no exception. I stopped on the bridge crossing the mighty Tweed and delved in the panniers to find my accommodation list and the map for the location of my B&B. Across the bridge, up the hill and left under the railway line. Easy. Surely I could remember that? Well, I must have been tired, or the rain on my specs was obscuring my view or something but, whatever the reason, I got lost. No surprise there then! As my friend and walking companion, Chris, used to say, I was suffering last mile legs. The cycle ride up the hill seemed arduous but eventually I found the tall, stone built terrace where the Bed and Breakfast was located.

A heavy wrought iron gate barred the entrance to a steep flight of steps up to the long front garden and a path the door. Not wishing to leave my bike on the street I heaved it up the steps and along the garden path to the front door where I rapped loudly on the knocker. A light appeared cutting through the gloom in the leaded fanlight above the door, and shortly after the door itself was opened by a pleasant middle aged lady. The usual introductions ensued and then she asked me to take my bike back down the path and the steps and wheel it round the end of the row to her secure garage at the rear. The words 'secure garage' mitigated the fact that I had to heave it back down the steps. She was waiting in the garage doorway when I arrived with the bike a couple of minutes later. Removing the panniers, I followed her through a door at the rear of the garage and into the large Victorian terraced house. More steps followed, three flights in fact, until she finally showed me into a guest room at the front of the house.

"What time would you like breakfast?" she asked.

"Is eight o'clock okay?" I asked tentatively, aware that some guest houses balked at anything earlier than half past eight.

"Oh, yes, that's fine. I'll leave you to it then. I expect you're ready for a cup of tea."

"Thank you, yes," I replied, wondering if I was about to be invited back down all the stairs for a cuppa (and maybe some cake)?

"The hospitality tray is on the dresser next to the window. If you need any more milk just give me a shout."

Okay, so no invite for cake – not such good news for my stomach, but better news for my knees! The door had barely closed behind her before I was switching the kettle on and examining all that the hospitality tray had to offer. Lots of tea bags: good. A little jug of fresh milk, still with condensation clinging to it: excellent, no nasty little UHT cartons! And best of all a Tupperware container full of a variety of biscuits: oh, yum!

I drank tea, ate biscuits, had a long hot shower and hand washed that day's clothing, hanging them over the radiator in the en suite shower room to dry. The rain was lashing against the window, not tempting me out but I needed to find something to eat. Hoping it might ease off after a while, I switched the television on, just in time to catch the news and weather report. The forecast for the next few days was mixed. Tomorrow was likely to be a mixture of sunshine and showers. The day after promised to be drier, the day after that better still and the day after that (the day I would be back at work) was promising to be best of all. Well, ain't that always the way? I growled in frustration at the man from the Met Office, and my stomach growled in frustration at me. Yes, time for tea.

Grabbing my purse, the keys to the front door, my cagoule and a spare carrier bag I set off down the stairs and into Berwick. It was barely 7 p.m. but was as dark and miserable as a damp late autumn evening. Berwick seemed to be deserted; not, I hoped, a portent of things to come – surely Berwick wasn't the Borders capital for stag and hen parties? Surely it wasn't all about to kick off later? Hopefully not, although from the way the wind was gusting and chasing clouds inland across the black waters, any party goers were likely to be in for a wet and windy night, wellingtons and sou'westers would be what they needed not high heels and blonde wigs!

I considered, briefly it has to be said, exploring Berwick that evening. The town was full of history and interesting architecture that I did not want to miss. But with the wind blowing and yet another shower blowing in, not to mention my stomach beginning to growl alarmingly, I decided to put off my explorations until the following day. So instead I explored as far as the nearest street with an array of eating establishments and homed in on a busy pizza parlour, the smell of garlic, basil and tomatoes enticing me into the steamy takeaway.

Generally, you can't go far wrong with pizza. Fish and chips can be more miss than hit: too greasy, soggy batter, limp chips and bony fish. Kebabs, especially the elephant leg variety – you know the thing – a huge lump of meat that can only be a reconstituted lump of something fleshy, possibly from more than one species (unless of course it really is an elephant leg) always leave me wondering what I might be consuming. Curries, I prefer to know the restaurant, too many horror programmes of vermin infested kitchens I think have put me off! But pizzas are usually safe.

Or so I had thought, until on a walking holiday a few years previously, when I found myself in a small town with only one takeaway and a couple of unappealing pubs. Standing in the takeaway, I had been about to order chicken and mushroom pie and chips, the most exotic thing on the menu, when I spotted a handmade sign blu-tacked to the wall behind the fryer, advertising margarita, mushroom and salami pizzas. I quickly changed my order to a mushroom pizza, only to watch in disbelief and dismay as one was grabbed out of a nearby freezer, unwrapped and frizz bee'd into the deep fat fryer.

There were no deep fat fryers in the pizza place in Berwick, so I could order with confidence. I spent the ten minutes I stood in the queue, reading the menu, reading it again, and wishing I had thought to pack a calculator. I was trying to do the mental arithmetic to work out if a nine inch Italian was better value than a small Hawaiian and a small Americano. As I inched ever closer to the front of the queue I began to panic that I had still not got the answer. Which should I choose? Large Italian with basil, salami, sun-dried tomatoes and olives? Or a small ham and pineapple and a small pepperoni? I fancied them all! And I was hungry enough that I would have a fair attempt at finishing them all too!

"What can I get you?" asked the hot young Italian behind the counter. (Okay, he was probably local, but I can dream can't I? And he certainly had the hot good looks of someone who had grown up surrounded by olive trees, mozzarella and pecorino)!

"A nine inch Italian, please," I replied, blushing as I realised just how it sounded. "Er, and a er, small garlic bread."

He grinned at me, as if it was the most normal thing in the world to have a blushing middle aged woman propositioning him for a pizza, and rang up my bill.

"Can I get you anything else?" he asked with a wink.

"No thanks," I squeaked, almost tempted to wink back.

Then he winked again and rubbed his eye and winked some more. At which point I realised his contact lens had come adrift.

With the hot, fragrant pizza boxes tucked safely into the carrier bag to keep the rain off, I hurried back to the B&B as fast as my legs would carry me. Juggling the boxes, trying to keep them flat, I fumbled with the key before finally opening the front door and hurrying furtively upstairs. I always feel a bit guilty eating in a guest bedroom, some places don't like it, and understandably so if your guests leave food stains on your soft furnishings as had been the case at the place in Seahouses. But I got to my room undetected, put the kettle on, made a pot of tea and sat down in the single chair, my lap draped with my fleece jumper to catch any spills as I tucked hungrily into the delicious nine inch Italian.

Just as I was taking a second bite, there was a huge flash of lightning and immediately a deafening clap of thunder. The pizza nearly stuck to the ceiling as I jumped in surprise. Fortunately for ceiling and stomach it didn't, and I finished off my meal watching a light show to rival any firework display as forked lightning shot across the sky and down to earth, hitting buildings, trees and even a street light.

Satiated with the garlic bread and the nine inch Italian, I drank some tea, munched a biscuit and then got ready for bed. Tucked up with a mug of hot chocolate I lazed sleepily, half watching a Whodunnit on television. There seemed to be far too many possible suspects for me to ever guess correctly and as the credits rolled I was still confused as to quite who had done it. Time to go to sleep I guess!

Chapter Four

"We serve a traditional Scottish breakfast," the landlady greeted me that morning as I stumbled sleepily into the dining room. "Will you be wanting everything?"

"Yes, please," I replied, wondering just what 'everything' was.

What did constitute a traditional Scottish breakfast? Porridge? Cullen Skink? Haggis? Neeps? Tatties? Oatcakes? Deep fried Mars bars? All washed down with a glass of Irn Bru and a whisky chaser? And more to the point: why? Last time I checked Berwick was still in England.

"Help yourself to cereal and fruit juice," the lady instructed, returning with a pot of tea which she placed on the table in front of me. "There's a good selection on the side board."

Standing up, I walked over to the sideboard. As far as what the traditional Scottish breakfast was, I soon had an answer. No porridge, or kidneys or kippers. Cornflakes, Shredded Wheat, Rice Crispies or All Bran. Hmm, All Bran: like food, only unappetising. I opted for that great Scottish stalwart: Rice Crispies. The cooked part of the breakfast was equally un-Scottish. Bacon, Lincolnshire sausage, scrambled egg (not fried?), plum tomatoes. Then came the toast and marmalade. Sadly not a Scottish orange in sight. Or even a Scottish raspberry in the jam. French preserves and Seville orange marmalade. And the toast was Blackpool milk roll. Not that I'm complaining! The French preserves were nice, the cooked breakfast delicious and I do love scrambled eggs, and the Blackpool milk roll really took me back to my teenage years when I spent my Saturdays working in a bakery that sold milk roll. But none of it seemed very Scottish to me. Maybe the landlady just did a good line in irony. She certainly did a good line in tea, when she saw me wringing the last dregs out of the pot she hurriedly refilled it for me.

As I had not had a chance to browse round Berwick the previous evening, I arranged with the landlady to leave my bike there whilst I went for a walk. There seemed little point leaving it chained to a railing somewhere in the town if it could remain secure and with the panniers packed in her garage. Taking a map of the town, I set off on foot. Whilst the weather was not too inclement I intended exploring as much as I could of this little town in this historic corner of England, or should that be Scotland, no England, no Scotland, no England... Well let's just say this town had had more border skirmishes and changes of nationality down the years than some parts of mainland Europe!

Berwick-upon-Tweed is now two miles from the Scottish border, but that has not always been the case. Before the border was ever fought over, as far back as Roman times, there have been settlements in the area. The name means barley farm on the Tweed, but you probably guessed the last bit! By the mid tenth century Berwick had become part of Northumberland and therefore England; but by the early part of the eleventh century it had become Scottish. It was made a Royal Burgh by Scot's king, David I, and in 1153 records show it was busy minting coins.

I could go on at great length about the English / Scottish Border Wars but it would take far too long and drag on a bit, a little like the wars themselves. Suffice it to say that the town changed nationalities a staggering thirteen times over the next four hundred years or so. Can you imagine trying to give directions to someone out of the area?

"When you reach the sign saying 'Welcome to Scotland' it's just a bit further down the road."

"Oops, sorry, all change! If you reach the sign saying 'Welcome to Scotland' you've gone too far. You'll need to turn round and go back a couple of miles."

"When you reach the dead blokes wearing kilts, bleeding in the ditch, you'll know you've arrived."

By the mid thirteenth century Berwick was a prosperous centre of commerce, well worth fighting over as far as the Scots and English were concerned, and was even being compared to Alexandria in terms of trading importance. All the to-ing and fro-ing and moving of the border signage finally came to an end, and the fighting became a thing of the past when the Act of Union was passed in 1707. But who knows? If the Scots gain independence in the future, as leader of the Scottish National Party, Alex Salmond, would like, it might all start up again! Better to cycle through it now while I don't need a passport.

The architectural legacy of all this is a town with earthworks, barracks, walls, towers and castles dating down the centuries. With information leaflet in hand, I wandered through the town that morning, following the history through the centuries, stopping to admire the grand ruins and the relics. From the top of the town walls I had good views over the harbour and river and down onto many of the buildings and old streets. One of the town gates, Mary Gate, stands at one end of the High Street. The walls were constructed in the Middle Ages and later strengthened during the eighteenth century. On the east and north side of town another wall, much stronger than the first and built during the reign of Elizabeth I, consists of huge stone bastions to house cannon and a large defensive ditch. From here I had good views of the coast and a football field which I would have thought would have proved more of a distraction to the soldiers than anything else; I'm surprised it was allowed to be placed there!

Soldiers manning the walls had been billeted in the town, but like modern day stag and hen party goers, they did get a bit rowdy. So, after many complaints from the poor put-upon townsfolk (well if it wasn't invading Scots, it was pissed up English soldiers!), in the 1700s a barracks was built to house the soldiers. Taking four years to build and finished in 1721, they are apparently the oldest barrack buildings in England. Built to house six hundred soldiers, the barracks remained in use until as late as 1965. It is now the home of the museum for the King's Own Scottish Borderers.

Opposite the barracks stands the parish church of Holy Trinity. It is a bit of a rarity, as it was one of very few churches built during the rule of Oliver Cromwell. Cromwell decreed that church bells should not be rung, as apparently it smacked a bit too much of the Roman Catholic religion, and he didn't like that! Anyway, he's dead now, and as if in defiance the church now has a bell, although it wasn't ringing as I walked past that morning, possibly because it was a Monday.

Bells he might not have liked, but Cromwell does not appear to have had any qualms about recycling (or should that be stealing?) stones from other buildings, although I don't suppose he personally oversaw the act. Holy Trinity, the nearby Town Hall and the barracks were all constructed using stones from Berwick Castle. Something that would never be allowed to happen nowadays to an ancient and historic building.

Dating from the twelfth century, and built during the reign of David I, the castle stands on a hill in the town overlooking the River Tweed. After a bit of a battering (and a change of nationality) it was rebuilt and further fortified by English King Edward I. Located at such a strategic position, it was much coveted and fought over during the Border Wars. It underwent a more agreeable change of ownership at the end of the twelfth century, when it was sold by Richard I to fund his crusades. A bit like stately homes being bought today by pop stars and Russian oligarchs, although in the case of Berwick Castle it was the Scots who were the purchasers. I guess they thought if they couldn't win it in battle they might as well wait until the current owners were a bit strapped for cash and then just offer them a silly price!

The castle declined in importance in the sixteenth century when further walls and ramparts were built around the town. Gradually it fell into decline, not helped by the barracks, town hall and church builders: so much for thou shalt not steal! Then came the railways. And there went the great hall and much of the other bits of the castle as the bulldozers moved in and flattened much of the place to make way for the railway station.

As I walked around the castle ruins that morning, all I really had to look at were the thirteenth century White Wall and the Breakneck Stairs, a steep and moss-covered flight of stone steps leading down towards the river. As far as trade descriptions and accuracy go, the wall isn't white anymore; however the stairs, as I nearly found to my cost, have been aptly named. They carried me down to the river – a little faster than I intended and with much wind-milling of arms and alarmed squeaks and curses – where the water was running sluggishly between the banks.

The River Tweed at this point on its journey is tidal. And as the tide was coming in, it was pushing the river back upstream in a daily battle of swirling currents and eddies. Tricky to cross, a rough wooden bridge had been built here in the Middle Ages; but thanks to a bit of moaning on the part of James VI of Scotland, who wasn't too pleased to find Berwick lacking a 'proper' bridge when he travelled through on his way to be crowned James I of England, a stone bridge was constructed. Mind, he didn't have it all his own way! It was twenty-one years before the stone bridge was built. Not that James got much use out of it, he died the following year. But everyone else benefited; Berwick Bridge is still in use, spanning the river on fifteen low arches.

In 1850, while one gang was busy knocking down the castle to make way for the railway station, Northumberland engineer Robert Stephenson, was busy building another bridge. This one was the Royal Border Bridge; it carries the railway over the Tweed, one hundred and twenty-six feet above the river on a series of twenty-eight arches, and was officially opened by Queen Victoria.

These two bridges coped with all the traffic into Berwick until, in the early twentieth century, it was deemed necessary to build another road bridge. The result, opened in 1928 by Vicky's great grandson, later to become Edward VIII, was the not very attractive concrete Royal Tweed Bridge. But at least it is still standing, unlike my local leisure centre that was demolished thirty years after it was built, when it was found to be suffering from concrete cancer.

The sky was like a bruise when I cycled away from the guest house later that morning. The same colour, in fact, as the bruises on my knees, a reminder of my fall the previous day and a further reminder to always make sure I had unlocked the bike before attempting to ride it!

Leaving Berwick, I was also leaving the coast part of the Coast and Castles route. Berwick also marked the one hundred mile point on the route, although I had cycled more than that due to getting lost and taking diversions. I had fifty miles to cycle that day to my goal, another B&B, at Galashiels, and for once the distance on the map and the distance I actually cycled were going to agree. Now there's a first!

Not a first was my encounter, yet again, with the A1 a couple of miles beyond Berwick. Until encountering the busy trunk road I had cycled on a main road up through the town and then a minor road followed by a short traffic-free path. With all care and diligence and heavy panniers, I carefully crossed the A1 to reach a minor road, roughly following the route of the River Tweed. A little way ahead Gainslaw Hill was marked on my map, I steeled myself for a stiff climb only to find it was a downhill! The route that day would take me on a few steep but mercifully short climbs, but nothing over two hundred metres. It would be the next day when I had my biggest climbs as I crossed the Moorfoot Hills.

Shortly after Gainslaw I reached Scotland. (If you are reading this after Alex Salmond has got his way and Scotland has gained independence, you might need to bear in mind the border might have moved south a bit or there might be kilted men with guns guarding the border, and a passport control office at this location). At the time of cycling there was none of these things, just a cheerful road sign informing me that Scotland welcomed me and five yards behind that another sign telling me I was entering the Scottish Borders.

Nothing looked any different, and indeed why should it? The road curved left ahead of me, on one side a dry stone wall with a grass verge coloured with pink flowers of red campion and white parasol-like blooms of hedge parsley. A young sycamore was in full leaf and next to it a hawthorn hedge full of white blossoms. On the other side of the road a neatly trimmed hedgerow of more hawthorn and stunted hazel bordered the road. A great tit called from the sycamore and a blackbird sang from the hedgerow.

A little way down the road and I reached a turn off for the little village of Paxton and close by, Paxton House. The gatehouse alone looked imposing and as for the house, situated in rolling parkland running down to the bank of the Tweed! Neo Palladian in style, it was built by architect John Adam between 1758 and 1763 for a rich young Scot called Patrick Home. The young buck had recently inherited the family seat of Wedderburn Castle, and having just come back from a Grand Tour of Europe he was brimming with fancy ideas. So with his new found wealth he commissioned the building of Paxton House. But with too much money and not enough sense, he lost interest before he had even moved in, and Paxton House was subsequently sold to his cousin Ninian Home. (I'm not making that up, he really was called Ninian). Ninian, with no less money but as it turns out much less good luck, set about adding to the opulence of his new humble abode by commissioning Chippendale to furnish it. But he did not live long enough to feel the benefit, he was killed whilst serving as Governor of Grenada, and so Paxton House and all his nice furniture, carpets, curtains, cups and saucers passed to his brother. The house remained in the Home family until a trust was formed in 1988, since when the eighty acres of park and woodland and the house have been open to visitors. Much work has been done to maintain the estate for wildlife conservation, including the erection of hides and nest boxes and land management to encourage a rich diversity of flora and fauna including deer, woodpeckers and the elusive waxwing.

If I was hoping to see any of this rich diversity of wildlife I was to be disappointed. I saw rabbits, some squirrels, lots of birds including a couple of noisy, chattering jays but no deer, or woodpeckers and certainly no waxwings. But the scenery was beautiful: rolling wooded hillsides, occasional glimpses of the majestic Tweed and copses of woodland carpeted by bluebells.

Paxton got me thinking of Paxman and Jeremy and the television quiz show University Challenge, of which Jeremy Paxman is presenter. But before Jeremy Paxman there had been Bamber Gascoigne, the question master in the original series. I had watched this as a teenager, forced to more often than not by my mother: "you might learn something!" In one instance she dragged me downstairs to watch the programme when I was trying to revise in my bedroom for my 'O' Level chemistry exam, so on that occasion I was actually less likely to learn something than my mum anticipated. But as a teenager I don't remember getting many of the answers correct; whereas now I manage to have a reasonable stab at answering many of the questions (with the exception of those concerning mathematics and classics). And the moral of this tangential tale? Well, it just goes to show that despite what they think, teenagers do not know everything! And mother doesn't always know best!

A few miles down the road from Paxton I got my first proper look at the Tweed since leaving Berwick. I had turned off the minor road onto an even more minor one running down to the river and the Union Suspension Bridge. At this point the river marked the border and I crossed back into England as I cycled over the bridge. As the Tweed meanders inland it continues to mark the border for many miles until just beyond Kelso.

The River Tweed, or Watter of Tweed if you're Scottish, or Abhainn Thuaidh if you're a Gaelic speaker (just rolls off the tongue, doesn't it?) runs for ninety-seven miles from its source on Tweedsmuir. The River Clyde also has its source on Tweedsmuir but that drains in the other direction to reach the sea beyond Glasgow. As the Tweed flows through the Border region it is fed by numerous tributaries including the comically named Blackadder Water. For much of its route from Berwick to Innerleithen sixty miles away, I would be shadowing Abhainn Thuaidh. Sorry, just wanted to imagine you struggling to pronounce it! I won't use the Gaelic form again – spellchecker hates it!

(But my Scottish travels have proved a continuous challenge to Microsoft spellchecker. For Abhainn spellchecker suggests Bahrain. It comes up with no offering for Thuaidh, can't say as I'm surprised! And it doesn't much care for Alex Salmond either (I'm sure it's not the only one) suggesting either salmon or almond (the damn thing's food obsessed). Leithen, a little further down the road, spellchecker thought would be much improved if changed to lecithin. And as for Newtown St Boswells, spellchecker was not impressed at all, but then neither was I having read its suggestion! Bowels! Oh yes, that famous Catholic saint: St Bowels, patron saint of I.B.S. sufferers).

The River Tweed is a world famous salmon fishing river. And the River Tweed Commission is the body responsible for preserving and increasing the river's stocks of not just salmon but sea trout and trout. As well as all the hands-on work of stocking the river, measuring and analysing it, the Commission also provides anglers with information via its website, information such as river levels, water quality and annual reports. Fishing on the Tweed is big business and a vital source of income for the local economy.

But the Tweed isn't just important for its salmon and trout. Because of the geology of the area, the water in the Tweed is clean and rich in certain minerals. Certain minerals that make it an ideal home for many invertebrates and crustaceans. And of particular ecological importance is the native white clawed crayfish. This small crustacean, similar to a little lobster, is very susceptible to pollution and likes a particular type of water quality. It can live in canals (if they are clean enough, so none in the Leeds and Liverpool in Nelson then), lakes and in well oxygenated rivers and streams, and it particularly likes limestone areas. Its distribution is mainly in the north of England and Scotland and if I was hoping to see any in the Tweed I would have to be extremely lucky (which I wasn't).

It is no surprise that I didn't see any, for starters they are nocturnal predators, emerging at night to feed on larvae, snails and aquatic plants. But more to the point these native crayfish are globally endangered and on the U.K. Biodiversity Action Plan as a priority species. So what has caused their near extinction? Loss of habit? Pollution? Predation? To some degree all these have had a part to play but the main culprit is a fella called Pacifastacus leniusculus better known as (and much easier to say) the signal crayfish.

Signal crayfish are one of six non-native species of crayfish that were introduced to Europe from North America in the 1970s. Originally farmed for food, the signal crayfish escaped and, capable of living up to twenty years, they are now widespread across Europe. Much larger and more aggressive than our native white clawed crayfish, they were soon out-competing their cousins. But size and violence were not the only reasons they had such an impact; they also carry crayfish plague, to which the white clawed crayfish is very vulnerable.

The lesser known Turkish crayfish was another foreign invader. Again, like the signal crayfish, the Turkish is larger than our indigenous crayfish but is not a thug, it is found mainly in the south and east of England.

While conservation bodies continue to protect and preserve our native white clawed crayfish its future is still far from certain. Signal crayfish are a popular delicacy and people do catch and cook them, after all that's why the blasted things were introduced in the first place. But beware! Don't catch the wrong one. Anyone found to have killed a white clawed crayfish is liable to prosecution and costly fines of several thousand pounds have been metered out to offenders found guilty.

I'm sure it was entirely coincidental, but shortly after crossing into England it began to rain, it continued to do so for the rest of the morning and well into the afternoon. I stopped and put on my cagoule; that was my upper body protected; my legs would just have to get wet. I cycled uphill, parallel to the Tweed for a short while before the minor road headed away from the river. Then came a relatively level and relatively flat stretch of road before a steep descent into Norham.

This was little more than a village by the Tweed; quiet, sleepy and with not a lot happening. At some point in the past however, much had happened here, as was evidenced by the sprawling ruins of Norham Castle. Battlements, castellated walls, a bailey, archways and arrow slits were pretty much all that were visible as I cycled past. Back in the twelfth century, the Bishop of Durham founded a castle here, commissioning a keep and bailey to defend his lands and property in the northern parts of Northumbria. The castle occupies a strong and strategic position, sitting as it does on the southern bank of the Tweed on a steep slope above the river, with a deep ravine on another side and the remaining sides protected by a moat. It has been besieged a staggering thirteen times, and can claim to be the most attacked of all the Border castles assailed by the Scots. King David I was one of the first to capture it; busy chap obviously. After all this assault it wasn't looking too great and underwent considerable restoration in the fifteen hundreds.

As I cycled through the village I spotted a cycle route sign and without thinking turned left in the direction indicated. I was now on Route 68, which was sixty-seven too many. What had happened to Route 1? The answer was simple, (a bit like my brain at that point). Route 68 joined Route 1 at Norham and headed south towards Haltwhistle, a fact my map illustrated if only I had thought to look at it sooner! Route 68 was the Pennine Cycleway and would have eventually taken me to Derby had I carried on going. I waited until a car had passed then did a U-turn in the road and cycled back to the junction where I had to wait for a gap in traffic before I could turn left and back onto Route 1.

"Idiot," I said to myself, as I sat at the junction.

"Pardon?" said an indignant young man, also waiting to cross.

"Sorry, not you. I was talking to myself," I attempted to explain hurriedly, hoping to avert any cross border conflict.

He gave me a glare and muttered something under his breath which sounded a bit like 'English butter', before crossing the road and disappearing into a shop. I really ought to stop talking to myself.

Keen not to make any more silly mistakes I took more notice of the map and the street signs and thus, a few short yards later, managed to avoid cycling down the dead end lane and into the river, as shown on the map. Instead I bore right, crossed the Tweed and the border once more and cycled uphill into Scotland. Quiet junctions and convoluted lanes running between grassy fields and passing small copses of woodland carried me roughly south-westwards, which seemed at odds with my eventual goal of Edinburgh to the northwest.

The river and the town of Coldstream were now below me to the south, and at a crossroads I turned left, taking the link route to reach Coldstream. I cycled one way along the main street, slowly spinning along, taking in the architecture of the stone houses lining the road. When the buildings began to peter out I turned round and cycled to the other end of the main street, stopping to look in the church and to read about the town in the tourist information centre. Not only was there much of interest to read about but it was warm and dry inside, giving my legs and feet a chance to dry and warm up a little.

In the eighteenth and nineteenth centuries Coldstream was to the eastern border what Gretna Green was to the western end of the England / Scotland border. On a main route into Scotland, it hosted the weddings of many eloping couples. But the town has been around a long time and someone else who headed through with war, rather than love, on his mind was English King Edward I. He marched through here to invade Scotland in 1296, and like many of these border towns Coldstream witnessed lots of to-ing and fro-ing during the Border Wars.

But this now quiet little town is more famous, not for that war but rather for a regiment. For Coldstream is synonymous with the Coldstream Guards. The regiment was founded in 1650, during the English Civil War (a brief period in history when the English actually stopped fighting the Scots and started fighting each other), as part of Oliver Cromwell's New Model Army. I don't wish to disparage the regiment but you could arguably describe them in their early years as a bunch of turncoats! By 1660, Cromwell was dead, and the English monarchy was restored; the son of King Charles I, whom Cromwell had had beheaded, was crowned Charles II (not much imagination these English royal families sometimes!) and the Coldstream Guards swore allegiance to the Crown.

Today the Coldstream Guards are still in existence, unlike some regiments who have suffered at the hands of budget slashing modern Governments. The regiment forms part of the Household Division, the Queen's personal troops, charged with guarding the reigning monarch. The regiment consists of six hundred infantry men, one hundred men who make up the Ceremonial Company (they are the ones with the red tunics and the Bearskin hats, and very hot heads, I shouldn't wonder), and the bandsmen of The Band of the Coldstream Guards.

Back on the official cycle route once more I was faced with a further series of small roads with little traffic, a few hills and much rain. I cycled along, the standing water on the road surface susurrating under the wheels, the sound a constant accompaniment on my journey that morning.

At Homebank, nothing but a couple of dwellings, I briefly touched the busier A road, rounding a bend in the route before heading north, away from the Tweed to the marginally larger settlement of Eccles. The name served to remind me that it was lunch time and I was getting hungry, although this Eccles is not the birthplace of the cake of the same name.

As Kelso hove into view in the valley, I took the link road to it, passing the race course on my way into the town. It was described by none other than Sir Walter Scott as 'the most beautiful if not the most romantic village in Scotland'. I can't vouch for the romantic part but it was certainly very picturesque. In the centre of this historic Borders market town I dismounted and wheeled the bike along the lanes and through the square. Evidence of Kelso's trading past were present all around me in the old street names: Woodmarket, Horsemarket, Mill Wynd, Coalmarket and of course (where would Scotland be without them?) Distillery Lane. Kelso market square is apparently the largest in Scotland and as I squelched my way around it that damp midday in June I could certainly testify to its size. Sadly most of the old buildings have gone, replaced by rows of Victorian and Georgian ones. The abbey, or its remains at least, are still here; founded in 1128 it stands on the northern bank of the Tweed on a bend in the river on the south side of the town. Kelso can also boast a castle but unlike some I had passed this one was a youngster by comparison; Floors Castle is visible from the bridge across the Tweed and stands out proudly and pronouncedly on the wooded hillside overlooking the Tweed, the town and the countryside to the south. It is not difficult to believe its claim that it is the largest inhabited castle in Scotland, and it is home to the tenth Duke of Roxburghe.

I was wet, I was cold and I was hungry. A choice of refreshment options was open to me: pubs, bakeries and a tea room. The tea room overlooked the square: a little building, possibly originally a house, it had a small neat garden at the front surrounded by a wrought iron railing. Tables and chairs were set out on the lawn, all empty thanks to the weather. I chained the bike to the railing, left my helmet hanging from the handle bars and took my purse and phone into the steamy tea room.

The interior was warm and humid and immediately the lenses of my glasses fogged up. I blundered into an umbrella stand in the entrance way, nearly knocking it over as I struggled to see through the fog. Taking my specs off didn't improve things much and I walked short sightedly into a table. I stopped before I risked knocking a pensioner flying or something, and tried to dry my specs on the very damp handkerchief I pulled out of my cagoule pocket. That didn't really help, so then I resorted to wiping my specs on my cycling leggings: no, no better. I unzipped the cagoule and next tried wiping them on my cycling top, but as that is made of stretchy synthetic material that didn't help either. What did I have that was dry and cotton? One thing and one thing only: my knickers! As I could hardly start wiping my specs on them I would just have to manage with either foggy focus or no focus at all. With my specs in one hand and the other stretched out in front of me, I shuffled slowly into the front room of the tea room, screwing my eyes up to try to focus as best I could.

I must have looked a bizarre sight: damp, squelching in my trainers, helmet hair in its usual disarray, groping myopically and pulling an odd face. A few teenagers huddled around one table all glanced in my direction and began sniggering. A young toddler burst into tears, but that might just have been a coincidence. A middle aged couple got up and left. Which was handy, and I immediately floundered over to the table they had just vacated and slumped into a seat. I shuffled off my cagoule and hung it carefully over the back of the chair, as I was sitting fortuitously next to a radiator the jacket would hopefully be dry by the time I came to put it back on. The cycling gloves I placed on top of the radiator, from where they began to emit an unpleasant odour as they dried, although at the time I just put it down to the mulligatawny soup that a chap at the adjoining table was noisily slurping from his spoon.

Picking up a paper napkin I dried my glasses and thankfully returned them to my face. I perused the menu, spoilt for choice between toasties, jacket potatoes, hot soup, cold sandwiches, quiches and salads. Not salad weather I decided, ruling that out, and the soup of the day didn't smell too appetising to me, so that ruled that out.

A waitress appeared at my elbow, and glanced pointedly at the puddle forming behind my chair as my cagoule continued to drip.

"Are you ready to order?" she asked.

"Oh, yes please," I smiled apologetically. "Could I have the jacket potato with tuna mayonnaise? A pot of tea and treacle tart please."

She scribbled something on her pad and disappeared. She returned barely a minute later with a pot of tea, cup, saucer, jug of milk and a jug of hot water. In my opinion you can judge a tea room by whether or not they serve a jug of hot water with their tea. A jug of hot water not only means I can drink more tea but that I can get it just how I like it: not too milky, not too strong and plenty of it!

"I'm sorry but the tuna mayonnaise has run out," she informed me.

"Oh, okay, then could I have cheese please?"

"What with?" she asked.

"Er, well some butter and maybe some baked beans too, please?"

At which point the waitress looked a bit puzzled. "On their own?"

"No, in the jacket potato," I replied, feeling equally puzzled.

"The potatoes have run out," she clarified. "The bread hasn't though."

"Okay, well in that case how about a cheese and ham toastie?"

"Oh, sorry, I'm not allowed to have lunch until the lunch time rush is over."

"What?" I asked in utter confusion.

"I canna have my lunch yet."

"Oh, I see! No, I meant for me."

"Ach! Sorry! Yes, I see what you mean. Okay." And with that she returned to the kitchen.

My toastie arrived five minutes later, with a nice accompanying side salad, which I hungrily finished off, even if it wasn't salad weather. The toastie was delicious and I managed to do what I always do with toasties, and burnt my mouth. I was halfway through my pot of tea when the waitress returned.

"Can I get you anything else?" she asked, clearing away the now empty plate.

"Yes, please could I have a slice of treacle tart?"

She bustled away with a clattering of crockery, returning a minute later.

"Sorry, the treacle tart has run out!"

"Apple pie?"

"None left, sorry."

"I don't suppose you do lemon meringue pie do you?" I asked hopefully.

"Ach! Now you come to mention it…"

"Yes?"

"No, sorry."

"Perhaps if you tell me what you have got," I suggested tentatively.

"There's clootie dumpling," she offered.

"Is that to go with the soup?" I asked, never having heard of a clootie dumpling and imagining something savoury sitting on a pan of meaty broth.

"No, it's made from suet and breadcrumbs and fruit and flour and spices and it's boiled for hours in a cloth. It's a traditional Scottish recipe."

She wasn't really selling it to me. The deep fried Mars bar sounded much more appealing as far as traditional Scottish food went.

"Thanks, I think I'll just have a scone."

"Would that be with cheese, fruit or plain?"

"Fruit, please."

"Jam and butter or jam and cream?"

"Jam and butter, please."

She hurried away, returning yet again in record time. I half expected her to tell me ach, there were no scones, but that was clearly not the case. Placing the bill and a plate bearing a huge scone, a mound of butter and a vat of jam in front of me, she hurried off.

Lunch in that tea room was one of the highlights of the trip. The huge pot of tea, the colossal scone, the delicious toastie and the slightly dippy waitress, combined with the fact that I had had a cold, wet morning and was able to dry out and warm up in comfortable surroundings were something I deeply appreciated.

The waitress returned just as I was hoovering up the last morsel of scone from my plate. I had the money ready, waiting on the table and handed it to her.

"Thank you," she said, taking the cash. Then, looking a bit embarrassed and nodding in the direction of the radiator, she added: "I think your gloves might be burning."

"What! Oh, giddy aunt," I cried, swallowing the expletive that was about to burst out of my mouth.

The gloves had more than dried on the radiator, they had toasted and were now rather crispy and rigid. I burnt my fingers removing them from the radiator and had to carry them from the café wrapped in my cagoule to protect myself from further burns. Outside by the bike, I unlocked it, put my cagoule and helmet on and wafted the gloves about to cool them before trying to put them on. Once on I was unable to flex my hand, it was like wearing strait jackets for the fingers! I took them off and beat them against the railing, not out of temper you understand, but just to try to put some flexibility back into them. The beating didn't do much other than get me a few funny looks from passing pedestrians. So I tried a different method, flexing and bending the gloves between my hands. There was a sound of something snapping which stopped me in my frantic finger flexing. I looked at the gloves, turning them over to try to place the source of the snap. A finger dropped off and fell to the floor.

"Oh, bugger! You stupid idiot," I said to myself.

I picked up the finger and put it in my pocket. Would it sew back on? A bit academic whether it would or not as I had not thought to pack a needle and thread, costume failure was not a contingency I had considered when planning the trip. In the end, ironically, the only way I found to soften the gloves was to soak them in water, so I might as well have not dried them in the first place!

Softened and soggy but flexible once more, the gloves still had a few hard crispy bits of melted nylon but at least they would offer some protection if I fell off the bike. Making sure I wasn't about to do just that, I double checked I had unlocked it, before mounting and cycling out of Kelso.

Leaving Kelso I had just short of twenty miles to cycle that afternoon. The sun was winning its battle with the rain and the afternoon was set to be fair and quite warm. At least the gloves would dry, although hopefully not formed to the shape of the handlebars! There always seems to be a hill after lunch, that day was no exception. May's Rule: the more you've scoffed, the steeper the hill. I cycled away from Kelso, up the hill, into the sunshine and through a changing landscape where rolling countryside gave way gradually to narrow valleys cut through with rivers and streams. Small copses of woodland dotted the landscape and I inhaled the delicate scent of spring as I passed many of these copses where bluebells carpeted the woodland floor. In the distance, and slowly getting ever closer, were the Eildon Hills and beyond those were tree covered slopes and the Moorfoot Hills.

Most of the route stuck to the minor roads, offering pleasant cycling with only a little traffic to spoil the peace. However, occasionally there were bigger roads to cross like the trunk road at Newtown St

Boswells. But before that there was a steep descent to Dryburgh, the village and the abbey of the same name, and the River Tweed once more. I crossed the river on a footbridge this time, pushing the bike over the glassy, slow flowing water, peering down off the bridge into the dark depths, hoping but failing to see white clawed crayfish. I did see some small fish however, although as to what species – salmon or trout – I have no idea.

It has to be said I was encountering as many abbeys as castles on this part of the ride, and the one at Dryburgh, although little more than a collection of crumbling ruins, has a long and interesting history. It was founded in 1150, which seems to have been a popular century for abbey founding. King David I (yes, him again) allowed the monks to take the timber from his lands but by all accounts they led a rather poor existence. Dryburgh was not one of the wealthy abbeys like those at Melrose and it seemed to suffer quite a bit of bad luck with its benefactors and bequests, not helped by being slap bang in the middle of all the land contested during the lengthy Border Wars. By the late thirteenth and early fourteenth centuries, the monks had wised up and seen which way the power struggles were going, the abbots submitted to English King Edward I and as result had their lands restored.

From abbey to saints as I reached Newtown St Boswells, not a town and not even very new. Records date the village to at least the 1500s. With lots of streams flowing in close proximity to it and the Tweed on its doorstep, the village was an important centre for corn milling, the monks of Melrose Abbey being just some of the customers bringing their grain to be milled here. With the coming of the railways it became a centre of livestock exporting and played an important communications role in the Borders region. The railway has gone now and so have the mills.

After Newtown St Boswells and its busy main road I enjoyed an all too brief section of gated road. Whilst the gates were a nuisance, having to stop, get off, open the gate, wheel the bike through, close the gate and cycle off again, this was more than made up for as the road was traffic-free. It skirted the eastern side of the Eildon Hills, made up of a series of three round summits, the nearest of which was the site of an ancient hill fort and earthworks.

I was now on the outskirts of Melrose. According to the notation on my map, improvements were planned for this part of the cycle route, but in the meantime I found myself once more crossing a main road to follow another quite busy road into the town.

Melrose is not especially large, but for centuries it was an important place. And despite its size it was certainly busy that afternoon as I cycled bumpily across the unevenly surfaced main square and through the town on a confusion of narrow one way streets filled with traffic and lined with parked cars. Melrose is a lovely collection of small independent shops, sandstone buildings and, of course, the magnificent abbey.

I planned to divert off the official cycle route in order to have a look at the abbey which sits imposingly on the eastern edge of the little town. The abbey is a must on many tourists' lists of places to visit in the Borders region, and it was easy to see why. The ruined mellow red stone building towers into the air, with graceful arches and a host of intricate stone carvings that vary from the carved windows and lintels to the fascinating variety of gargoyles.

It was founded by, yes you've guessed it, King David I (busy man) in 1136 and was the first Cistercian abbey in Scotland. Tourists can make a beeline to the spot where the heart of Robert the Bruce is buried, although if they want to pay homage to the rest of his body they'll have to travel to Dunfermline Abbey. Melrose Abbey and the abbey church were of great importance both spiritually and politically, a fact that resulted in many attacks by the English down through the centuries. Both Edward I and Edward II had a go, and then Richard II had an even bigger go in 1385 which resulted in virtually the complete rebuilding of the abbey church. So it comes as no surprise that very little of the original abbey church remains, with most of the present building dating back to the time of the rebuild, but despite that it is claimed to be one of the most magnificent of all the medieval churches in Britain, and considering just how many there are, that's quite something!

There were a lot of people milling about and not many of them seemed to have any road sense, several times I had to swerve, brake suddenly or ring my bell as people stepped out into the road or generally hurled themselves under the front wheel. Why was it so busy? As I cycled past the abbey I had my answer. A notice displayed events happening for the Queen's Golden Jubilee. That was today! Caught up in my own cycling holiday I had completely forgotten about the Jubilee and the celebrations that would be taking place up and down the country. I'm not a Royalist but I had been happy to take the additional bank holiday granted for the Jubilee and thus save a day of my leave entitlement to have sufficient time off work to cycle the Coast and Castles.

It was not too many miles now until I would reach Langlee and leave the cycle route for that day, taking instead a link route into Galashiels. The toastie and scone seemed but a distant memory as I cycled along the valley bottom, following the river, not the Tweed this time but Gala Water, one of its tributaries, into Galashiels.

I had no map or directions for the B&B, just an address, which was a bit of an oversight on my part. Galashiels is not big, but it's not that small either, and as I cycled into town I realised, with a sinking heart, that the guest house could be anywhere. I would have to ask for directions. There was a petrol station just up ahead so I pulled in to ask. I might as well have talked to the petrol pump for all the help the scruffy youth behind the counter proved to be!

"Dunno, soz," was his considered response to my enquiry.

I cycled away, hoping for a shop or a dog walker or a policeman or a street map of the town to appear. Just as I was beginning to get desperate something better than any of those overtook me and then pulled in to the kerb fifty yards ahead. Someone got out of the back seat and walked away, and I hurried to reach the car before it set off. I had just found a taxi! And who better than a taxi driver to know where a particular address was?

"Excuse me," I said, hurrying up to the driver's window and tapping on the glass.

The window descended to reveal a figure sitting, I say sitting, it was more poured, into the driver's seat. With a huge belly completely hiding the seat belt and thrusting up against the steering wheel, tattoos colouring both beefy forearms, various bits of metal and stud work piercing ears and nostrils, a skinhead haircut and a studded collar around the neck, the driver was the sort of man your mum would warn you not to get into a car with! I was beginning to regret my decision when the driver spoke, belying all the judgements and prejudices that had just popped into my head.

"Aye, can I help you?" asked the taxi driver, in a soft female voice.

"Yes, if you could please," I stammered in surprise. It was a woman!

"I'm looking for this B&B." I offered the paper bearing the address through the window.

"Ach, you're nearly there," she smiled. "Just carry on going up this road for another couple of hundred yards and it's on your left. It's a whitewashed hoose with a blue front door. Ye cannae miss it!"

"Oh, that's great. Thanks very much," I replied, grinning.

"If you want, I can chuck your bike in the back and give ye a lift. Free of charge, mind," she added with a smile.

"Thanks but it's not far, I'll be fine. Thanks for your help."

I set off feeling somewhat belittled. The taxi driver could not have been more helpful and friendly. It was a reminder not to judge people by their appearance. And I had to remind myself that most people probably took one look at me and thought 'mad, unkempt idiot with a bike' or 'English butter' or something along those lines! Although, come to think of it, they'd be right!

The whitewashed B&B with the blue front door was just as the taxi driver had said, a little further up the road. An elderly lady answered the door to me and showed me, bike, crispy nine-fingered gloves and all into the hallway.

"You can leave your bike here, it'll no be in the way," she said. "I'll show you to your room."

I had chosen this particular B&B out of necessity. When planning my trip I had been unable to find much accommodation in the Galashiels area that I did not immediately rule out on the grounds of either location (like a noisy pub) or financial (like expensive hotels and travel inns). This B&B was reasonably priced and advertised itself as cyclist and walker friendly. Plus the breakfast had sounded good!

My room was on the first floor; I felt my knees saying a quiet thank you to the god of stairs. A family room, I had a choice of a couple of beds, so naturally I plumped for the comfiest which also happened to be the double. There was a hospitality tray with a goodly selection of tea bags and a couple of sachets of instant hot chocolate but sadly no biscuits.

"Your bathroom is just down the landing," the elderly lady pointed a shaking hand in the direction of several doorways. "What time would you like breakfast?"

I was tempted to say 'in ten minutes' as I was once again ravenously hungry, but restrained myself and asked if eight o'clock was too early.

"Ach, no, that's fine. We're early risers. I expect you'll be wanting to get on your way."

"Yes, I'm cycling to Edinburgh tomorrow," I explained.

"Oh, well, you'll be needing a good breakfast then," she beamed. "I serve a full Scottish breakfast. Will you be wanting everything?"

"Yes please," I replied greedily.

As the lady left me to the kettle I could not help but remember that I had heard this full Scottish breakfast spiel before, and been disappointed to find it no different from the English version. Would this B&B be any more Scottish I wondered? Well, this time I was actually in Scotland, so that was a start! Porridge? Oatcakes? I began to fantasize. But then, as I was pouring boiling water onto the teabag, a thought occurred to me. What if kippers were part of a full Scottish breakfast? Or, worse still, smoked salmon? I don't like oily fish, to the extent that the taste makes me want to retch. What would I do if I was confronted with a steaming plate of Arbroath smokies the next morning? Or scrambled egg adulterated with smoked salmon? Could I smuggle them out in the rear pouch of my cycling top? Maybe I could take the plastic bag lining the litter bin down to breakfast and hide them in that, then flush them down the loo later? Or maybe I could just man up and – no, not eat them! – just admit I didn't like them? This was the sort of embarrassing problem I could lie awake worrying about! And knowing me I would! I decided the best course of action was to go down and ask the lady if fish featured on her full Scottish breakfast menu. So I did. And I was much relieved to discover it didn't.

The cups of tea did much to refresh me but I needed some food, but before that I needed a shower. Taking clean clothes, the towel and my toiletries I made my way down the corridor to the bathroom. It was a shared bathroom, not the luxury of an en suite, which is always more convenient especially if I need the loo in the night. But shared bathrooms do often have one advantage, especially if they are shared with the home owner, and that is there are usually toiletries provided, which is not always the case with en suite facilities.

This bathroom had a large bath with a shower over it and lots of toiletries: shampoos, conditioners, shower gels and bubble bath. I ran a bubble bath and whilst waiting for it to fill set about doing my laundry. The timing was good: laundry done as bath reached a reasonable level. This time I didn't plunge straight in, I checked the temperature first. Confident I wasn't about to strip the skin from my body I climbed in and relaxed under the bubbles.

Within ten minutes my muscles and aching knees were feeling much better, and I was bored. That's the thing about baths, whenever I think 'ooh, a long hot soak would be nice' I find that within quarter of an hour of starting said soak I've got fed up and want to get out. I should have taken a cup of tea and a book with me! Not that I find it easy to read in the bath – yes, you've guessed it – my specs steam up!

Feeling bored but relaxed, as per advertised on the bottle of bubble bath (the relaxed bit, not the bored bit, I can't imagine the tag line 'be bored in the bath' would do much for their sales figures), I stood up, pulled the plug and decided to rinse off and wash my hair under the shower. With the shower running I reached for the bottle of shampoo, peering myopically at the label. Duly shampooed and rinsed, I then reached for the bottle of conditioner. It didn't match the shampoo. Not a cardinal sin or anything but I always buy matching shampoo and conditioner. The shampoo had been apple flavoured, although when a few suds got in my mouth they certainly didn't taste like it! But the conditioner smelt of lemons, odd but not an unpleasant smell. The consistency though, once I had rubbed it all over my head, was certainly odd! It didn't feel like conditioner feels, it wasn't silky on my luscious, greying locks. In fact, to be honest, it felt more as if it was stripping my hair than conditioning it. Making sure none was about to drip into my eyes, I reached for the bottle and squinted at the label.

"Removes limescale and freshens as you clean," I read slowly and with escalating panic. "What?! Oh, sodding hell! Crap!"

Which, as it transpired, was an apt choice of expletive. I had conditioned my hair with bathroom cleaner. Lemon scented bathroom cleaner admittedly, but nevertheless bathroom cleaner.

"Shit!" I was on a lavatory based roll now! "Shitting shitty crap!" I squealed, as I ducked back under the shower, frantically rubbing my hair under the running water and keeping my eyes and mouth tightly closed.

Fifteen minutes I stood under that shower, rinsing, shampooing, rinsing, conditioning (with the proper stuff this time – I even put my specs on to make sure), rinsing, re-shampooing, rinsing and conditioning again. Yes I had wanted clean hair; but limescale-free hair? That was going too far. Well, I shouldn't have a problem with dandruff! Dermatitis maybe, but not dandruff.

When I eventually turned off the shower, wrapped myself in a towel and stepped out of the bath I was frightened what I might find staring back at me in the mirror. Well, let's be frank, it's never that great! But I was concerned the bathroom cleaner had been a bleach based product. I might have gone blonde! Worse yet, I might have gone neither one thing nor the other! Or even ginger! Or green! Or I could have stayed mousy brown with aspects of grey! The creature staring back at me wasn't ginger. Or green. Or platinum blonde. Just plain old mousy brown with aspects of grey. But despite the subsequent rinsing and washing and conditioning it was evident from the matted thatched pan scourer appearance of my hair that the bathroom cleaner was powerful stuff. I'm used to bad hair days; every day is a bad hair day as I have fine fly away hair and not much patience when it comes to taming and styling. But this looked like an uncoordinated, blind chicken had been trying to nest build! Looking on the bright side, it could have been so much worse: right next to where the bathroom cleaner had been sitting was a bottle of toilet cleaner and that promised to kill 99.9% of all germs. And that could only mean one thing. Bleach!

Back in the bedroom I tracked down a hair dryer in the chest of drawers and went into battle with brush and comb. It had all the makings of another epic border war. It was like trying to brush long, shaggy Velcro and as for combing! Teeth snapped and pinged across the room as I attempted to haul the comb through my hair. After an arduous ten minutes, the comb was missing twelve teeth, and lots of scrabbling about on my hands and knees only resulted in me finding eleven of them. I gave up the hunt, and dried my hair. The creature staring back from the mirror looked like she had cycled through many, many hedges backwards. I tried to console myself that some young trendies would pay a fortune for the same windswept, distressed look I had just achieved for free after thirty minutes and liberal applications of bathroom cleaner. But even the moneysaving aspect of the consolation failed to console. But there is one thing to be said for having weirdly, startling hair, after a while, because you can't see it, you kind of forget about it.

Although as I set off into the centre of Galashiels a little while later in search of some food, my hair raising incident was still, at that time, very much on my mind. I needed some painkillers, having forgotten to bring any and wondered if, on this bank holiday evening, I would actually find any shops open. I was in luck. The first shop I came to was a late night chemist. I went in and began browsing the shelves but was quickly distracted by the hair care products. The variety of hair colorants was staggering, as were the prices. People paid this much to go a colour the manufacturers inventively called 'apricot' but which looked to me like Satsuma orange? And as for 'sunset Carmen' that was warning triangle red as far as I could tell from the picture on the packaging! Had I ended up with bleached hair I would have wanted a colour to take my hair back to its normal shade. But, looking along the lines of boxes, that was a tint the cosmetic houses clearly didn't do. There was nothing called 'rodent bronze' or as I would call it mousey brown. Nor a variation on that such as 'degu alloy with highlights of argent' or the more truthful light brown, generously streaked with middle aged grey. After fifteen minutes of reading the packaging and all the various instructions – and I had thought A Level chemistry had been challenging at times – my stomach rumbled loud and long, reminding me there were more important, and infinitely more interesting things, than hair dye.

In the centre of Galashiels I found a town square laid to lawn and flower beds and surrounded on a couple of sides by shops, pubs and takeaways. One of the takeaways was busy and from it there wafted the enticing aroma of garlic, basil, tomatoes... Yes, it was another Italian takeaway. Some things you cannot have too much of. Chocolate is one. Cream cakes another. Well-conditioned hair a third. And pizza definitely a fourth. Okay, so I'd had pizza the previous day. So what? I joined the queue and spent a contented few minutes just inhaling the appealing smells.

No fit, young, virile Italian this evening. The guy behind the counter certainly looked Italian, but it was more in a Marlon Brando, Godfather way, than an Italian stallion kind of way. Whatever, he was a good advertisement for his pizzas, if the way his rotund belly straining against the striped green, red and white apron he was wearing, was anything to go by. You probably won't be surprised to find I was ravenous. For food that is.

"Garlic bread, large meat feast and a portion of salad please," I said, when I reached the front of the counter.

"Okay, you wanna the large garlic bread or the small garlic bread?" he asked.

Gosh, he really was Italian, I thought. "Large please." (Come on you didn't expect me to go for the small did you)?

My order was filled a rapid five minutes later and I hurried outside to sit on an empty park bench overlooking the flower beds. It was the warmest part of the day, the sun had come out, a group of lads were playing football and showing off to a group of girls lounging nearby on the grass, families were strolling about and a few early Jubilee revellers were already heading into the nearby pubs. A blackbird was searching about in the flower borders for worms, tugging frantically on one as he tried to pull it out of the soil, and house sparrows hopped about under the benches on the lookout for any dropped crumbs. If a chicken came past I was ready to pull my hoody up before she could lay an egg on my head!

The foot long garlic bread was a French stick, not, as I had been expecting a flat pizza base with garlic butter smothered all over it, but it was delicious. The pizza was equally delicious and the healthy portion of salad well, it was healthy but still very good, packed as it was with black olives and red peppers. An hour later, the football game had concluded, the sparrows had eaten quite a lot of garlic bread crumbs and the families had gone home. Feeding the empty food wrappers and boxes into a litterbin, I too went home or at least back to the B&B. I was feeling pleasantly full and had quite forgotten about my hair raising experience.

Television offerings that evening consisted of soap operas full of people shouting at one another, Scottish dancing and on the remaining channels wall to wall Jubilee and Royal documentary programmes. Sitting waiting for the kettle to boil, I flicked through the channels, dismissing each in turn. I picked an individually wrapped teabag from the hospitality tray and added the boiling water, then while it brewed, I read through the T.V. guide. There was nothing on. Not an unusual state of affairs. The only thing I was remotely interested in was an old black and white Jimmy Stewart movie, it was one I had seen before but I didn't mind that. What I did mind was the dreadful reception on that particular terrestrial channel and after suffering a couple of minutes of snowy vision where Jimmy's blurred outline had a double shadow, I gave up and switched the set off.

I removed the teabag, absentmindedly added milk to the cup, gave it a perfunctory stir and settled down with my less than thrilling paperback thriller. To be honest, the instructions on the backs of the packets of hair dye had been more thrilling and I was beginning to regret not choosing a different book to bring. I turned the page and took a sip of tea and was transported straight back to the bathroom!

"What the…?" I spluttered, coughing tea back into the cup.

It tasted awful. Yes it looked a bit milky, but that wasn't the worst of it. There was a sharp and clashing taste of lemon. Plonking the cup down, I poked about in the litter bin for the tea bag wrapper. In trying to multi task – make a cuppa and see what was on telly – I had picked up a bag of lemon and ginger tea and not noticed. Normally I like lemon and ginger tea, it's quite refreshing. Just not with milk. Lemons and I were not getting on well that evening. I hastened to the bathroom, poured away the tea, refilled the kettle and then returned to my bedroom. With the next cup I made sure to concentrate on the job in hand. Darjeeling, milk, no sugar, no lemon, no ginger. No wonder friends and relatives worried about me going away on my own!

Chapter Five

"Ye'll be wanting a bowl of porridge?" the landlady asked, as she served me a pot of tea (sans lemon and ginger) at the breakfast table that morning.

"Oh, yes please!" I happily agreed.

The porridge duly arrived, hot, steaming and with verbal instructions to help myself to syrup, sugar or salt. You could be a bit too Scottish, I decided, opting for syrup instead of the traditional Scottish salt. The porridge was delicious, especially with a copious quantity of syrup, and I had barely finished it before the lady reappeared to whisk my empty bowl away and replace it with a large, steaming plate of Scottish sausage, bacon, two fried eggs, Scottish black pudding, baked beans, mushrooms and tomatoes.

"I'll be back in a minute with some toast," she told me, hurrying away into the kitchen.

As good as her word, a minute later she returned, but not just with toast, there was a plate of oatcakes, a jar of Scottish raspberry jam and another jar of whisky marmalade. I could get very used to these Scottish breakfasts.

"Did ye sleep well?" she asked, returning to replenish the toast rack with more hot toast.

"Yes, thanks, the bed was very comfy," I replied truthfully.

"Aye, only you have a look that you tossed and turned a bit," she smiled, her eyes straying to my hair.

That morning, apart from the shade, it was doing a fair impression of boxing promoter Don King's, and I had awoken to find the missing tooth from the comb embedded in the hair at the nape of my neck. Well, at least I found it before someone else did!

"Oh, my hair has a mind of its own. One of us has to!" I added ruefully.

The sun was poking through a watery sky as I set off down the hill and through Galashiels that morning. The forecast had been for a drier day than previously but with the potential for a few showers, although the first one wasn't to hit me until mid-morning.

Galashiels is first referred to around the time of King David I (there's no escaping him) and has long been an important and strategically placed border town. By the sixteenth century it had become an important centre in the textile industry, standing as it does on Gala Water, and during that period there were three fulling mills in the town. The plentiful supply of wool came from the numerous flocks of sheep grazing the nearby hills. The coming of the railways had an impact on the town's textile industry as it meant transport costs were reduced and also brought in cheaper wool from elsewhere. But by the end of the nineteenth century the wool industry was in decline; and the First World War only served to hasten the decline as many young men from the town, including many mill owners' sons and mill employees rushed to enlist at the outbreak of war.

During the first years of the war, when there was a surge of patriotic volunteers clamouring to answer Kitchener's cry and enlist, regiments were created from local areas – Pals Regiments as they came to be known. The idea was the camaraderie of men with a common background, serving together, would achieve a stronger regiment; and it undoubtedly did. Whole groups of friends, brothers, cousins and colleagues enlisted together; there were even sportsmen, schools and stockbroker battalions. But the dreadful reality of Pals regiments was that entire towns were often affected by the sudden and single loss of their young men. Eventually in January of 1916 this policy was brought to an end, but it was too late to stop the horrendous loss suffered by one of the most famous of these Pals Divisions – the Accrington Pals. Their fame was borne of terrible tragedy. On the first day of the Somme offensive in the summer of 1916, 720 men of the Accrington Pals went over the top. Within the first twenty minutes 235 had been killed and 350 were injured. By the end of the day 584 were listed as killed, wounded or missing. Accrington, Burnley, Galashiels and too many other towns throughout the country suffered similarly because of these Pals Divisions and the heinous stupidity of war. Of the Galashiels Pals, over 600 died during the Great War, many of them during just one battle at Gallipoli.

Textiles still have a role to play in Galashiels. The town is home to Heriot-Watt University's School of

Textiles. By the 1960s electronics companies and local Government were providing much employment. In recent years, where once the fulling mills stood, there has been much redevelopment to provide the ubiquitous retails parks and commercial developments attracting national chains of supermarkets, shops and restaurants to the town.

Galashiels might never have been famous for its fulling mills, and it certainly won't be for its retail parks; however, the annual celebration, known as the Braw Lads Gathering, brings tourists to the town in large numbers every year. The Braw Lads take their name from the Robbie Burns poem, and the gathering has been taking place since the 1930s; but its origins go back much further than that celebrating, as they do, the granting of the town's burgh Charter in 1599. Additionally, the Gathering celebrates (or commemorates depending on your nationality) the events of 1337 when locals killed English raiders caught in the act of stealing plums. The modern day Gathering consists of Braw Lads (and Lassies) journeying through town on horses, carrying flags, trotting across the river Tweed and visiting various places and people of note in the Burgh, all to the accompaniment of a marching pipe band and lots of flag waving. The poignant culmination of the day's ceremony sees the Braw Lads and Lassies honouring the town's dead at the War Memorial.

It seemed appropriate that I found myself singing 'Brothers in Arms' as I rejoined the main cycle route on a minor road that hugged the banks of the Tweed. I was now cycling in a south-westerly direction,

which seemed at odds with the north-westerly
direction in which Edinburgh lay, but the route was
soon to twist away to the north. The river at this
point was considerably narrower than it had been as it
flowed down from the Southern Uplands. Soon I
reached the confluence of the Tweed and another of
its tributaries, Ettrick Water, and beyond it the Tweed
shrank even further. The hedges and wooded
hillsides were in full summer green leaf: hawthorn,
beech, blackthorn and ash contrasting with the darker
needles of the distant forestry plantations on the
hillsides. I couldn't see any plum trees, just as well
perhaps, as the picking of any wild fruit could get a
Sassenach into all kinds of trouble in these parts!

Several cars, with mountain bikes mounted on their
roofs or boots, overtook me. They must have been
heading for the nearby Yair Hill Forest to enjoy a few
hours of blasting round the cycle trails there. It was
some time before I reached the entrance to the forest
car park myself, having risked the off road route
highlighted on my cycle map, that skirted the eastern
edge of the hill.

According to the map, this off road route would avoid
a busy section of main road near the small village of
Caddonfoot, but the map also warned this off road
alternative was not suitable for heavily laden touring
bikes. Just how did they define heavy I wondered? I
weighed no more than nine stones, my panniers
although full were not so heavy I risked a hernia
every time I tried to lift one. Surely the combined
weight was still considerably less than some heavily
built cyclists? And I was not actually on a touring

bike, I was riding a hybrid which, with its wider tyres and suspension seat post, was designed to be ridden on a variety of surfaces from tarmac to tow paths. I decided to chance the off road section, gambling that unless it involved muddy sections, big boulders, drop offs, steps and angled duck boards I should be okay. And as it transpired I was okay, the worst parts were a short section coated in an excess of loose gravel and a near miss I had with a large, steaming pile of horse muck.

Running along a valley with hills on either side, the next few miles were relatively easy, level going. But this was to change at Innerleithen where I left the Tweed, turning north and now following the tumbling Leithen Water up into the Moorfoot Hills. A long but steady climb faced me, and initially I was hampered by the first shower of the day. Cagoule on, I sweated my way up a couple of miles of quiet minor road but soon the sun was breaking through and a tail wind was chasing the clouds away to the north, and giving me a helping push up the hill.

I was part way up the steady incline, working my way towards the Moorfoot Hills, when I heard an electronic chime indicating an incoming text message. Reading the text seemed like a good excuse for a break, so I slowed to a halt (which didn't take long) and climbed off the bike. The text was from a friend, Tracy. I had remembered that earlier in the year she had stayed in a holiday cottage on the route, and had texted her to see whereabouts it had been. At the time of sending the text I had thought I had just cycled past the potential cottage and so had come to a halt, sent the text and then sat down to await her reply, deciding to eat a bar of chocolate while I waited. Tracy had replied, dispelling my notion that I may have cycled directly past the front of the cottage, as it turned out to be not quite where I had thought. But in typical Tracy fashion she had replied two days after I had sent the text! Fortunately for both my time schedule and my waistline I had given up waiting for a reply after fifteen minutes and just the one bar of chocolate.

I passed Whindlestraw Law on my right as I continued my wind-assisted progress up the hill. Now the route was running alongside the tiny Dewar Burn, the water appeared dark as if stained by the peat bogs as it drained through the moor. Soon I was descending to Garvald Lodge but the respite for my legs was brief before, once again, I was faced with a steep climb, passing Whiteside Law and Longshaw Law. Many of these hills were called Law, nothing to do with legal matters, just a Scottish word for hill.

The Moorfoot Hills make up part of the Southern Uplands, a range of hills that have their own National Trail – the Southern Upland Way – running through them. This National Trail   passes through Galashiels and no doubt many walkers make that little town an overnight stop on their route, just as I had done. The Moorfoot Hills themselves stretch north eastwards from Peebles and into Midlothian and form part of the catchment area for the River Tweed. Comprising of folded bands of sedimentary rock, the topography consists of a biologically diverse and environmentally important mixture of landscapes that include bogs, marshes, grassland, heath and moorland. On the higher parts the wild heather moorland dominates, whilst on the foot hills of the Moorfoot Hills grassland is predominant. The Moorfoot Hills may not rival the height of the Scottish Munroe's but the scenery was wild and beautiful. The highest point is Whindlestraw Law; at 2162 feet it is only a few hundred feet higher than Pendle Hill near my home, and many of the fauna and flora of the two areas are similar.

Lining the road in some parts were clustered mounds of bilberry, their delicate and tiny deep pink flowers hiding amongst the rich green leaves, promising an abundant bilberry harvest to come later in the summer. Bilberry crumble has to be one of my favourite crumbles, but the fruit are so tiny and hard to pick that for two hours work I'm not inclined to share the resulting crumble with anyone! The heather moorlands would be a mass of purple later in the year, but as I cycled past on that early summer's day the heather had yet to flower. I heard grouse calling a warning to one another from some parts of the moor but despite searching I failed to see any. Lapwings however, I saw aplenty. With their distinctive 'peewit' cry a flock of them swooped and flew in formation above me. A curlew cried and flew overhead to land adjacent to the road, staying long enough for me to get a clear photograph of this brown speckled bird with the curving beak. Skylarks sang and so did I, but nowhere near as tunefully.

The morning rolled on, a long but steady hill climb; and with the sun shining and a constant tail wind it was a pleasant cycle ride. The scenery was beautiful and there was plenty of it to admire as I cycled towards Edinburgh.

Suddenly the climb was over. I reached the edge of the Moorfoot Hills, the land dropping away to the northwest, a landscape filled with fields bisected by tiny streams (or burns to use the Scottish term) and speckled with small, odd-shaped plantations of coniferous woodland. On the horizon the city of Edinburgh was tucked between the Firth of Forth and the countryside, with the mound of Arthur's Seat guarding the city to the east. Beyond the Firth of Forth the mountains of Fife, in Central Scotland, were visible on the horizon.

I slipped over the edge of the hills, a wonderful free-wheeling descent leaving the moorland landscape, passing through scenery of green fields bounded by dry stone walls where sheep grazed, rabbits nibbled the grass and more curlews cried and flew overhead. The road I was on was quiet enough, but at a tiny crossroads the route turned left, onto an even quieter country lane. Still descending I crossed Middleton South Burn and was suddenly confronted with a flock of sheep blocking the road.

Several dozen sheep (I tried to count them but they wouldn't keep still long enough and I nearly nodded off in the process) and their lambs, were making a slow progress in my direction, in no particular hurry as they stopped to stare at me. Those on the edges of the flock took full advantage of the roadside's grassy verges and hedges to nibble the lush grass and young leaves of the already closely cropped hedge. Behind the flock, an equally laid back farmer sat in his Land Rover, quietly herding the sheep towards me. I stopped and put both feet down, the sheep hesitated and then first one brave sheep and pretty soon the entire flock passed me in a skittering rush of cloven hooves, woolly fleece and much bleating. The farmer nodded at me and raised a hand in thanks as he slowly brought up the rear. I nodded and smiled in return. My smile soon slipped when I noticed the road ahead. It was lavishly pebble dashed with sheep poo. Too much to avoid, and I cycled stickily through the mess, poo clattering up against the mudguards and getting wedged between them and the tyres.

"Could be worse," I muttered to myself in consolation. "He could have been moving some cows!"

It was a short, steep, smelly and mucky climb into the collection of dwellings at Middleton. It was nice to know that apart from one little blip before Edinburgh there were no more uphills! The gentle downhill now required some pedalling unless I was to coast into Edinburgh some twenty miles further on considerably later than intended (like the next day)! But it was a fabulous ride of narrow quiet lanes, fields, hedges, stone walls and, every so often, wooded copses crowding in over the road, creating green, leafy tunnels of bird song that I cycled happily through. Sunlight flashed and glinted through the leafy canopy but the weather was far from hot and I continued to wear a jumper and long cycling leggings.

As I neared Edinburgh the countryside was rapidly running out, but traffic-free paths gave me a gentle introduction to the encroaching towns. Bonnyrigg and Lasswade came and went on a pleasant traffic-free couple of miles. But then came Dalkeith and the busier main roads of the town as I carefully negotiated my way along Eskbank Road and the High Street. The map notations showed a tantalising possibility of traffic-free cycling if the Borders Railway Line re-opened, but at the time I was cycling that had yet to happen. A roundabout and then a toucan crossing which, if you don't know, is like a pelican crossing but designed for both pedestrians and cyclists, marked the edge of town and from there I returned to traffic-free bliss on what did indeed appear to be part of an old railway line on the Penicuik – Musselburgh Foot and Cycleway. I shared the route with other cyclists, some of whom appeared to be commuting home from work, and pedestrians.

Before reaching Musselburgh the cycle route to Edinburgh swung off to the west, skirting Portobello, the seaside resort to the east of Edinburgh. The next few miles were all traffic-free and for much of the way were on the old Innocent Railway Path, passing through residential areas, but this brought its own hazards. Litter, check. Broken glass, check. Deaf pedestrians who couldn't hear my bell, check. Dogs running about off the lead, check. Two small children swinging a hefty chunk of two by four at my bicycle, check.

Okay, that's a first even for me. I've been sworn at by drunks, sworn at by angelic looking little girls, spat at from the top deck of a school bus, sworn at by bad drivers, chased by geese (they can't half shift and those long necks give them a distinct advantage when it comes to reach), I've even had someone on a bus throw an egg at me (fortunately it missed). But never before have two small boys under the age of four (or anyone, come to think of it) tried to knock me off my bike with a plank of wood.

They must have been hiding behind a bush or something, because one minute I was dreaming of what to have for tea that evening and the next two scruffy little oiks and one enormous chunk of wood were hurtling towards me! I resisted the urge to scream 'it wasn't me eating the plums' and instead settled for something more assertive but possibly just as ill thought out!

"If you hit me with that," I bellowed, "I'll knock you into next week!"

Quite how I would have achieved that physics-defying bit of time travel, I'm not sure. But the two little thugs obviously believed me. Their jaws dropped, and so did the plank, and I pedalled rapidly away. Maybe they were the next budding Burke and Hare!

Edinburgh was within reach and the impressive mound of Arthur's Seat, rising to a height of over two hundred and fifty metres, was just ahead. Long before the city had sprung up there had been Bronze Age settlements on Arthur's Seat and when the Romans arrived in the first century there were already

Celtic tribes living there. The hill is dotted with earthworks and the remains of old hill forts, enclosures, hut circles and ancient cultivation terraces and the ruins of the old Saint Anthony's Chapel, as well as a network of footpaths and interesting sounding places like Sainsbury Crags, Gutted Haddie and Cat Nick. The land is now part of Holyrood Park, on the northern side at the foot of the hill stands the Palace of Holyroodhouse and the remains of the twelfth century Holyrood Abbey. Arthur's Seat was one of those places that deserved longer to explore than I could spare it and I decided I would have to come back when I had more time to see the sights not just of Arthur's Seat but of the city itself.

I cycled around the south western side of Arthur's Seat, the hill rising above me on the right, before entering a tunnel that spewed me out a short while later into the bustle and hubbub of Edinburgh. This was where I left the cycle route, my hotel was a short distance away on Dalkeith Road, all I had to do was find it! I had a name and a street number for the hotel and had assumed it would be relatively easy to cycle along Dalkeith Road until I reached the correct number. But I had reckoned without the busy teatime traffic and the sheer length of Dalkeith Road. It was some time before I tracked down my hotel for the night.

Staying in a city is always going to be more expensive than in towns or rural villages and a capital city even more so. After much researching of cycle friendly accommodation in the city, I had dismissed the hostels as being potentially noisy, dismissed many

143

of the guest houses and B&Bs as being too far from my route, and dismissed many of the hotels as being too posh, too expensive and likely to look less than kindly on a sweaty cyclist arriving and expecting them to accommodate not just cyclist but sheep poo-covered cycle. In the end I had booked what I considered to be my best option: a family run hotel, not too far from my cycle route and not too far from the city centre but not too near as to be prohibitively expensive. That said, I was still paying considerably more than at any of the previous places I had stayed.

Chaining the bike to the railings, I took mobile and purse and went into reception to register. With that out of the way I was shown outside and round the back, across a cobbled yard and to a garage where I could leave the bike. I chained it up, removed the panniers and wandered back to the front of the building to be shown up to my room by a tartan-skirted lady. The lobby was quite opulent and somehow seemed all very Scottish: deep red, Paisley patterned carpet, polished wood panelling and solid dark oak staircase. The walls were covered, above the panelling, with dark patterned wallpaper and hung with oil paintings depicting views of Edinburgh. At a bend in the stairs a stained glass window let in the mellow afternoon light to fall colourfully on the carpet and walls. There seemed to be a lot of stairs before we finally reached a room where the landlady produced a key and ushered me inside. I guess single rooms are few and far between in many hotels and this one seemed to have been crammed into a nook in the eaves. There was a single bed, covered with tartan throws and pillows, a bedside table containing

144

lamp, Gideon's Bible and hospitality tray, a single wardrobe squeezed into a narrow alcove and a panelled door into the world's smallest en suite shower room. The shower room consisted of the world's smallest sink, a toilet (the size of which I had not seen since nursery school) and a very narrow shower cubicle. On the plus side the hotel room was clean and comfortable and the bathroom sported the world's fluffiest towel and a good selection of Scottish heather flavoured toiletries.

I made a pot of tea, ate a Scottish shortbread biscuit, then ate another, slipped out of my trainers and cycling gear and then squeezed myself into the shower room to luxuriate in a long hot shower. Better not eat too much that evening or I may not be able to fit back into the en suite, I thought! I lost count of the number of times I whacked my elbows on the sides of the shower cubicle before getting out and continuing to whack my elbows on the walls as I towelled dry and combed my wet hair before squeezing out of the shower room and back into the bedroom. With pins and needles running down both arms from all the hits my funny bones had taken, I dressed, ate another biscuit (living dangerously I know) and then set out into the bright lights and big city of Edinburgh.

My knees were aching after another day of going round and round, a sign, according to all the cycling literature of an incorrectly adjusted saddle, or more likely in my case, encroaching middle age and over use.

"If you find cycling makes your knees ache, your saddle may be too low, so try raising the height," declared Dr. Bike.

Carefully following all advice on correct saddle adjustment, I had found that my knees ached after a long day, regardless of the height of the saddle. If I raised the saddle any more I would be unable to put a toe to the tarmac and in danger of keeling over. Any higher a sitting position and I might as well convert to a penny farthing!

So it was with less of a spring in my step and more of a lurch in my knees, that I hobbled down the stone stairs from the hotel entrance and onto the pavement that evening. My hotel was three miles or more outside the centre and I stood at a bus stop trying to make sense of the timetable. I failed miserably and decided to walk instead. An hour later I reached the centre of Edinburgh. After fifty-three miles of cycling and an hour's walk I didn't really feel like walking round the city centre as I had originally planned. But then I spotted a city tour bus, engine running, idling at the kerb on the other side of the road. Watching for traffic, I dashed across and leapt on board just before it set off. What a fabulous way to see the city and learn a little of its story. With the earphones clamped to my head, I lost track of time as the bus took me round the city, showing me the sights whilst, in a gentle Scottish brogue, a voice in my ear narrated the history and culture of Edinburgh. Sitting on the top deck, with my fleece jumper and cagoule zipped up to my chin to protect against the cool wind, I was able to look down on many of the buildings and courtyards, and was on eye level with scores of the beautifully detailed shop and pub signs we passed. I peered over tall walls into hidden closes, squares and graveyards, all the while listening to tales of murderers, heroes, ghosts and grave robbers. We drove past the castle, the railway station and along Princes Street and the Royal Mile lined with shops selling everything from kilts and whisky to books and cute furry haggis.

The sun was casting long shadows, lighting up the roof tops and silhouetting the castle and church spires as it slowly sank that evening. As the day cooled off it didn't deter the numerous pedestrians as they swarmed the pavements and sat at trendy pavement cafes. Traffic clogged the roads and tourists wandered, cameras at the ready, snapping away at the castle, the buildings and even the open top tour bus. By the time the bus disgorged me back where I had started, my head was spinning with the sights and information I had taken in, and my stomach was rumbling from lack of food.

Having been sat down for most of the day and still in awe of the bus timetables, I opted to walk back to my hotel. My feet were aching as the hotel came in sight and I had still not had anything to eat. A tempting smell of garlic and spices wafted under my nose from a neighbourhood Chinese takeaway and my feet carried me with suddenly renewed energy into the pungent interior. I hurried out not long afterwards with a set meal for one. I had been tempted by the set meal for two but remembered the miniscule en suite and thought better of it!

Back in the hotel, I once again felt guilty about taking food up to my room but no one was about and I reached the room undetected. I put on the kettle, switched on the television, spread the takeaway cartons on the bedside cabinet and spread my cycling jumper over my lap and the bed as I propped myself up against the headboard. And that's when I remembered I had no cutlery! The first part of the set meal was easy – finger food in the form of prawn crackers and spicy pork balls with a sweet and sour dipping sauce. The special chop suey and egg fried rice proved more of a challenge.

"Julia, you're an idiot," I muttered, as I cast about the bedroom looking for inspiration.

Could I use my tyre levers, I wondered? Bit narrow, and in any case they were in the puncture repair kit in the saddlebag on the bike. Could I fashion a plastic spoon from the lid of the sweet and sour carton? Fashion it with what, my teeth? Fingers! I would use my fingers, invented before cutlery, how else had Homo sapiens fed himself until some bright spark thought 'I know I'll invent the fork?' Have you ever tried eating rice with your fingers? I gave up after the first mouthful missed my mouth entirely and cascaded down my T-shirt to land in my lap. At this rate I would need the ground sheet of a six person tent over my lap and the rest of the room to catch the mess! I put the food to one side and made a cup of tea while I considered the problem. It was only as I stirred the milk into the tea that I realised I was holding a spoon!

"Julia, you're a genius," I said gleefully. Okay, perhaps genius is a bit strong for someone who was all set to use tyre levers to feed herself with just a minute ago!

So I happily watched the news and weather, and then happily (and very appropriately) watched the old classic black and white film 'Whisky Galore', and happily ate my Chinese meal. Slowly, with a teaspoon. Replete with beansprouts, chicken, prawns, beef, pork, onions, shredded carrot, peas, rice and monosodium glutamate, I carefully picked up all the litter and, making sure to bag it all up securely, I deposited the empty takeaway cartons in the bathroom bin. Now thirsty from the excess of sodium all Chinese takeaways seem to specialise in, I made another cup of tea, which I soaked up with another shortbread biscuit, or two.

A very young looking Gordon Jackson was at odds with various members of the cast, and an equally youthful James Robertson Justice kept popping up, whilst other members of the cast squabbled over the best places to hide their influx of whisky. Suddenly the film was interrupted, not for the first time, by another advert break. I'm not accustomed to Scottish adverts, and daft as it sounds there is a definite difference between English and Scottish television advertisements. Every second advert that evening seemed to be one sponsored by a health authority, NHS Trust or cancer charity. And all the others were advertising food and drink.

"Don't drink and drive!" exhorted a kilt-wearing Highlander, waving a claymore about menacingly.

The next advert featured a particularly well known Scottish game bird and lots of people merrily sipping whisky, which seemed completely at odds to me with the previous ad!

Next came something a little more in tune with the first advertisement. "Made in Scotland, from Girders," declared a man clutching a can of Irn Bru, standing in front of the Forth Railway Bridge. I've never had Irn Bru. What did it taste like? Should I try it whilst in the land of the fizzy orange stuff, I thought?

"When was the last time you had a well man check-up?" demanded a Rab C Nesbitt lookalike.

"Never," I muttered, although I doubt he heard me.

And then there was a shot of rolling hills, white cliffs, Blackpool Tower and Stone Henge; 'Greensleeves' played in the background and a posh English accent said, "Live it, love it, visit England."

"I will do," I promised the television. "Tomorrow."

Chapter Six

The shower room spelt pungently of Chinese meals
that morning. Too much spice in too small a space. I
left the extractor fan running as I went down to
breakfast, hoping that the cleaning staff wouldn't
think I had personally made the smell!

Breakfast, although Scottish, was nowhere near as
good as the Galashiels feast. There was porridge and
cereal and an interesting sounding concoction called
Cranachan. Consisting of oats, cream, raspberries
and whisky it sounded delicious, apart from the
whisky! I was tempted but I really don't like whisky,
so I stuck to safe porridge, making a mental note to
make myself an English version without the alcohol
as soon as I got home.

Edinburgh was bathed in sunshine as I saddled up and
set off later than morning. But a stiff breeze was
blowing, making the day seem considerably cooler. I
cycled back to rejoin the route and was soon ensnared
in one way streets, busy roads and pedestrian
crossings. I had two targets that morning, the first
being the end of the Coast and Castles Cycle Route at
The Mound in the centre of the city and near to the
castle; the second goal was North Queensferry, a
further twelve miles away, following the Edinburgh
to Aberdeen Cycle Route map. Where one cycle
route finished, the other started. I had the map for the
next cycle route and so was not anticipating too many
difficulties as I cycled into the city that morning.

With a population of nearly half a million, Edinburgh has been the Scottish capital since the fifteenth century, but it has, like so much of the Borders region, seen much conflict. In the seventh century the Borders were already being fought over and the Lothian region, in which the Borders and Edinburgh lie, came under the rule of King Oswald of Northumbria. But unlike the area around Berwick that continued its nationality tug of war for many centuries, Edinburgh and its surrounding area was reclaimed by the Scots for good in around 950 A.D.

Good old King David I founded the Royal Burgh of Edinburgh in the early twelfth century, the locals got on with life and peace reigned until the mid sixteenth century. In 1544, in a retaliatory attack, English King Henry VIII attacked the city. A royal marriage agreement between Mary Queen of Scots and Henry's son, Prince Edward, had turned sour, Mary had obviously had second thoughts and Henry was fuming! He ordered his invasion force to attack Edinburgh, and the city was taken despite English troops attacking each other at one point. But Edinburgh Castle, perched atop its rocky hill, put up a better defence than the city and whilst much of the city was destroyed the castle remained intact.

Edinburgh slowly rebuilt itself after Henry's scaled up temper tantrum. Eventually all the infighting and feuds of the English and Scottish monarchs became academic in 1603 when King James VI of Scotland (himself the great, great grandson of England's Henry VII) succeeded heirless English Queen Elizabeth I and was crowned James I of England. In 1707 the

Act of Union was passed, and the Scottish and English Parliaments were merged, creating the Parliament of Great Britain based at Westminster in London. This move was not, as you can imagine, as popular with the Scots as the English, and it was not until 1999 that Scotland once again got its own Parliament, although even then it was not fully autonomous.

By the eighteenth century Edinburgh was developing as an important banking centre, but like all large cities, alongside the wealth and opulence there was much poverty and overcrowding. Traditional industries of printing, brewing and distilling were the mainstays of the city's economy; but as the industrial revolution progressed Edinburgh's manufacturing sector increased to include rubber and engineering works, although unlike other cities in Britain, Edinburgh never became particularly industrialised.

By the twentieth century much of the slum housing was being cleared for redevelopment; there are a few residential tower blocks but not many, and many of the leafier suburbs are home to professionals living in much sought after architectural gems of Georgian and Victoria houses. The twentieth century also witnessed the growth of financial districts in the city, and many parts of Edinburgh have been transformed by the growth of business parks, as well as the expansion of the University.

Edinburgh is often compared to Rome, built as it is on seven hills, although possibly the similarities end there. But despite much redevelopment and new buildings, many of the older buildings remain. There are a staggering four and a half thousand listed buildings in the city, which gives you some idea of the history, heritage and importance of the architecture. The grand imposing stone buildings lining Princes Street hint at a city with a long and wealthy past. In the part of the city known as Old Town, which lies between Holyrood Palace and Edinburgh Castle, the roads and lanes still echo the medieval street layout. On the main streets that make up the Royal Mile there are tall old buildings, behind which are mazes of cobbled alleyways known as Closes. Nearby are more old buildings such as Saint Giles Cathedral and many of the older parts of the university. In 1824 fire rage through the Old Town, destroying some parts completely. Rebuilding took place on top of the old foundations, resulting in passageways and vaults being created under the Old Town. The East Vaults were created with the building of South Bridge Street. This whole area was designated a UNESCO World Heritage Site in 1995. It is now possible to tour some of these vaults – yet another reason for me to come back to this part of the world when I had more time to explore!

There was one place I did have time to look round and so I diverted to Greyfriars Kirkyard, or churchyard. Located in the Old Town, it has been in use since the late 1500s and was consecrated to replace the overflowing churchyard at St Giles Cathedral. There are many famous people interred there under the intricately carved gravestones and monuments and in the mausoleums, including the ninth Earl of Argyle and various scientists, authors,

154

churchmen and one William Wallace. Not William Wallace, trouble maker and Scottish freedom fighter, but William Wallace, mathematician. Personally I'm not sure which would be worse: a life full of difficult mathematics or a death of being hung, drawn and quartered! A hard one to call.

Possibly the most famous body buried at Greyfriars is not a human at all but a dog. Greyfriars Bobby was a loyal terrier who, for fourteen years, slept on his master's grave summer or winter, rain or shine and was fed by kindly locals. He eventually died in 1872 at the rather good old age of sixteen, and a statue of him was commissioned and placed at the corner of nearby Candlemaker Row. Books have been written and films made of this touchingly loyal little dog. But debunkers of this story claim the dog was just one of many strays that inhabited graveyards in Victorian times, fed by curates and visitors; one even claims that Greyfriars Bobby was replaced by a similar dog each time it died. Personally, I prefer the original if somewhat romantic version; plus it would be a shame to think that the red granite gravestone erected for Bobby in 1981 by The Dog Aid Society of Scotland had been wasted!

Wandering through the Kirkyard, morbidly reading the faint inscriptions eroded by time and pollution on the blackened headstones, I came across several sturdy metal cages. These are mortsafes. You've heard of anti-vandal paint? Well, mortsafes are anti-grave robber graves! Put there to keep the dear departed from becoming the cheap dissected.

With the growth of medicine and the profession of surgery becoming a respected trade instead of the preserve of the barber surgeon, the demand for cadavers for dissection had begun to outstrip supply by the late seventeenth and early eighteenth centuries. Anatomy schools had opened in many places where universities offered training for the growing band of doctors and surgeons, and Edinburgh was one of the leading cities in this discipline. Convicted criminals who were sentenced to death provided most of the bodies for the anatomists to practice their trade on and to pass on their knowledge to the next generation of doctors and surgeons. But sadly for the anatomists there were simply not enough convicts being hung to provide them with enough cadavers. And just as today, if a gap exists in the market there will be someone willing to fill it by whatever means possible, so it was in Edinburgh at that time. Anatomy schools were willing to pay for fresh cadavers and men were willing to provide them – even if it meant breaking the law to do so. Grave robbing became common practice in Edinburgh.

Heartbroken relatives would bury their relations one day, come back the next to lay flowers and find the grave had been opened and the body stolen. In order to avoid detection, grave robbers operated in gangs, posting lookouts, and going to many lengths to leave no clue of their nightly larceny. Some developed the knack of digging open only the head of the grave and then sliding the corpse out, leaving the majority of the soil undisturbed and the remainder needing very little tidying up to hide any sign that the grave had even been robbed. But the authorities, the churches and the relatives were wising up to the grave robbers: patrols were stepped up, and in many cases mortsafes were employed to prevent any attempt at grave robbing.

Even without these precautions, grave robbing was time consuming and rather hard work: all that creeping about at night, dodging the night watchmen, all that digging! Sometimes the corpses had started to deteriorate and anatomists were less than keen to pay for a partially decomposing body, understandably so.

But what could be better than a freshly dead body that you did not have to dig up after dark? Well, a freshly murdered one, that's what. Enter two Irish immigrants Messrs William Burke and William Hare. They had been employed as navvies, so should have been very good at digging, but perhaps they had got a bit fed up with that and fancied a change. After all, why dig up a body when you could just kill one? Spotting a niche market, these two men set about murdering a total of sixteen victims and selling their nice, fresh cadavers to Edinburgh anatomist Dr Robert Knox.

Life (and other peoples' deaths) was good to the two men, and their little body business was showing a nice operating profit until one day, they were caught by a suspicious lodger at the boarding house run by one of the pair. Well, you would be suspicious if you found a dead body at the place you were staying, I know I would be!

In the ensuing trial the two murderers contradicted each other and passed the blame so much that the jury was completely confused. As a result Hare was offered the opportunity to turn King's evidence, in effect giving him a 'get out of jail free' card, and he immediately did so. The men had been aided by Burke's mistress and Hare's wife but in the event both women were acquitted. Dr Knox, who Burke swore had known nothing about the origin of the bodies, was not prosecuted. Burke was found guilty and hung. And, as was custom at the time, his body was dissected. His death mask, a cast of his face after his execution, is now on display at the Surgeons' Hall; his skeleton is displayed at Edinburgh's Anatomy Museum. Rather a fitting end to the body of a man jointly responsible for so many deaths. Just a shame Hare got away with it!

Leaving the atmospheric Greyfriars Kirkyard, I cycled off towards the Mound and the end of that cycle route map. As I neared the Castle a dreadful screeching noise started up, sounding like an exceptionally asthmatic goose the noise quickly settled into a recognisable tune played on Scotland's most famous instrument, the bagpipes. Amazing how such a beautiful sound evolves from such atonal beginnings, and who was it who originally thought 'I know I'll connect a bladder to a collection of pipes with holes in them and try to play it'? Roy Castle? He could play a teapot!

I was instantly reminded of a friend's daughter who, on hearing bagpipes for the first time at the tender age of three, turned to her parents and asked: "Is that music?"

Before I spotted the Mound, I spotted (hard not to) Edinburgh Castle. The Castle dominates the city's skyline and is the setting every New Year's Eve for Edinburgh's Hogmanay celebrations. One of the most intact castles in Britain, it sits on top of an extinct volcano that was once the site of an Iron Age hill fort, and has been the location of many fortifications for hundreds of years, with buildings being added throughout the centuries.

Edinburgh Castle was, I'm sure you will not be surprised to learn, fought over by the English and Scottish during the Wars of Independence. Half the places I'd cycled through seem to have been fought over! As well as being the home of many Scottish monarchs, in the seventeenth century the castle became a military base and a jail. Our old friend Dave I built St Margaret's Chapel in the grounds, and other buildings making up the castle include museums, the Great Hall and the Royal Palace. In 1457, King James II was presented with Mons Meg, a huge cannon, by the Duke of Burgundy. Mons Meg still stands overlooking the battlements at Edinburgh Castle, but its firing days are over.

I found the Mound quite easily, sitting as it does in the shadow of the castle, and stopped to remove one map from the map case on my handle bars, fold it up and pack it into the pannier, and replace it with the second Sustrans map. This one I had actually been sent in error by Sustrans online shop and had been told, when I phoned them about the mistake, to just keep it and they would send out the correct one. So having ended up with a free map I had decided to make use of it, not by extending my cycling holiday to Aberdeen – I didn't have enough leave to allow time to cycle the further one hundred and seventy miles to the granite city – but I did have enough time to cycle onward, over the Firth of Forth and catch a train back over the famous Forth Rail Bridge. So that was what I planned to do that morning.

Following the new map, I set off down Princes Street, fortunately only for a short distance. The pavement was no less crowded than it had been the previous evening but there was certainly more traffic on the roads that morning. Cars, taxis, lorries and buses all revved and tooted and battled for space on the busy road. I kept a sharp lookout for any dangers as buses pulled out, taxis darted in and cars overtook me. It was with relief that I turned off onto a quieter side road and then shortly after turned again to cycle parallel with Princes Street along the less populous George Street.

George Street ended at Charlotte Square. A square of yet more heaving traffic that seemed to be on an endless conveyor belt round and round the square. It shouldn't have been claustrophobic but with the traffic, the looming dark buildings and the noise of roadworks, it was. I cycled round the square trying to do far too many things at once. Mind that car! Mind that bus! Mind that pedestrian! Mind that pot hole! Read the map! Watch out for road signs! Where were the road signs? Why couldn't I make sense of the map? Why had I not seen a blue cycle route sign on any of my three laps of the square? I was beginning to feel like a hamster on a wheel, going round frantically and getting nowhere. And unlike the hamster I didn't have pouches full of food to keep me going!

At the start of my fourth lap of what I was beginning to call Car Lot Square, I stopped, pulled the bike onto the pavement and carefully examined the map. According to said map, I should leave the square opposite the road I had entered it, down what appeared to be not a road but a passageway. Maybe that was why I had not been able to find my exit. Glancing at the map as I cycled along had made it appear that I turned off to the left down a road, so I had been looking for a road where none existed. I should have been looking for an alleyway or footpath or something. At that point I decided to walk round the square rather than get back on the bike and enter the traffic fray, in doing so I quickly found a blue cycle route sign tucked obscurely onto a lamppost and pointing down a lane to the left.

"Eureka, I have found it!" I cried, doing my best Archimedes impression.

A pavement artist, standing to the side of me, dressed entirely in grey and with grey face paint, fell off his pedestal in surprise. He gave me a dirty look (well a grey look at least), climbed back on his pedestal and assumed his frozen pose once more.

The lane carried me back onto more busy side roads and I found myself humming 'On Every Street' as I slowly negotiated traffic, map and junctions as I cycled north westwards out of the city. It was a convoluted route and I fully expected to get lost again but I didn't. Well, not there at least. But shortly after joining a traffic-free cycle path I reached a confluence of several cycle routes that was nearly my undoing. Vandals had been at work, turning the cycle route signs round on the lamp post. There were signs for Queensferry pointing back the way I had come from, signs for Glasgow, signs for Edinburgh, signs for Newcastle and several signs for different suburbs all pointing in various directions. One had been snapped off entirely and was jammed pointing downwards into a drain cover. That one summed up how I felt the ride was going at that point. I allowed myself the small luxury of a moment of panic. I had a train to catch. Miss it and it would mess up the whole schedule for getting back to Newcastle. If I picked the wrong route I could waste precious time and there was the potential to cycle many miles before I even knew whether I was going the correct way or not. Getting lost is not a new experience for me. But it doesn't get any easier to cope with. I was just contemplating the irony that there is never anyone around to ask for directions when you need them, when a cyclist whizzed past.

"Excuse me!" I yelled to his rapidly disappearing back. "Which way to Queensferry?"

He squealed to a halt, locking his rear wheel and leaving a black line of rubber on the tarmac.

"Sorry," I smiled apologetically. "The signs have all been moved round. I'm not sure which way I need to go to get to Queensferry."

"Ach, the wee beggars been at it agin, ha they?" he growled. "Need conscriptin', gee 'em summat te doo!"

"Yes," I agreed heartily, wishing he'd stop ranting and point me in the right direction.

"Ach, Queensferry, ye say? Weel now, tha'll be over yonder." He nodded his head down one of the cycle paths. "Cycling across yon bridge are ye?"

"Yes, that's right."

"Aye, well if ye see any more o' yon little buggars, ye'll do well ta throw 'em o'er yon bridge!"

"Yes, I might well do that," I agreed, although if they were armed with pieces of two by four it might well be me going for a swim.

"Where are ye from?" he asked. "Ye've a mighty strange accent."

"Burnley," I replied.

"Aye, that explains it!"

I could only agree with him. My accent has generally caused nothing but confusion and misunderstanding on so many of my travels around Britain, I was just lucky he understood me at all.

Thanking him for his help I cycled off towards Queensferry. The traffic-free route continued through numerous suburbs, often meeting other cycle routes but the vandals had not been at work at any of these and the sunny morning held no more dangers of getting lost. At Davidson's Mains I rejoined some minor roads for a mile or so and then was back on a track again, this time cycling through the middle of a golf course. The sea was getting ever closer as the route gradually drew nearer to Queensferry.

After Cramond Bridge, there was a mile or so of road cycling before I reached a track paralleling the busy A90. The Firth of Forth was somewhere not too far away on my right but the gently rolling, wooded parkland of Dalmeny House blocked the sea from view. Near the town of Dalmeny I stopped to take a photograph of the two famous bridges crossing the Firth of Forth. Seeing them for the first time in the distance, standing out above the tree tops and fields, and knowing I had nearly reached the end of my cycle ride filled me with a strange mixture of anticipation and sadness.

Anticipation and sadness were quickly replaced by disgust and annoyance as the cycle route suddenly became covered in broken glass. I hate litter, to me it is the epitome of laziness and irresponsibility. Not only does it mar the scenery, it can be polluting, harmful to wildlife and it is usually non-biodegradable, meaning it will remain in the environment often for decades if not centuries. Sweet wrappers, newspaper, takeaway cartons, plastic bottles, cigarette ends, lager cans, glass, the list is virtually endless. And please don't get me started on bags of dog dirt! Litter in towns is bad enough, but when it's in the countryside, somewhere you would only expect people who appreciate the natural environment to go, I find it even worse. Why carry something out for a walk or a bike ride and then not bring it back? (They wouldn't do that with anything else they were responsible for, like their granny or their children)! The number of discarded inner tubes I've come across in the middle of nowhere is amazing, who are these lazy cyclists who cannot be bothered to take the punctured inner tube to the nearest bin? The latest trend is energy drinks and energy gels (when did food stop providing energy? that's what I want to know) and now I find I'm coming across more and more discarded plastic bottles or plastic sachets that provided some much needed energy for a litter bug! What a shame these energy products don't provide just that bit more energy so they can be carried to a bin!

So, anyway, there I was on a cycle route surrounded by broken glass. There was just too much of the stuff to attempt to cycle through, so I got off the bike and carried it across, muttering all the way. I had barely cycled a couple of hundred yards before I met up with a cyclist who had obviously cycled through the glass. Her bike, a hybrid similar to mine but with considerably less sheep poo on it, was upside down and she was struggling to unwrap the rear wheel from the chain. Why is it nearly always the rear wheel that punctures?

"Hi," I called, slowing down. "That glass was dreadful wasn't it?"

"These paths should be swept regularly," she moaned. "I don't suppose you know how to change an inner tube do you?"

"Yes, I've had lots of practice," I answered wryly. "Would you like a hand?"

I parked my bike, took off my gloves and helmet and prepared to get covered in chain oil and brake dust. With our combined efforts the wheel came off easily enough, along with lots of dirty grease, and we set about removing the tyre and inner tube, chatting as we did so about cycling, broken glass and vandalism to the cycle route.

"I've been asking my husband to show me how to do this for ages, and it's one of those things he's never got round to doing," she explained apologetically.

"Well, you'll know for next time," I replied, rubbing a greasy hand under my nose without thinking. "The worst bit can be getting the tyre over the rim sometimes."

Tyre off one side of the rim and inner tube removed, I set about checking the tyre for more embedded glass and removing all that I found. It took a few minutes as there was plenty of it.

"You have got a spare inner tube, haven't you?" I asked, suddenly fearing the worst. I didn't mind helping change the tube but the thought of trying to find a puncture without a bucket of water was not comforting.

"Oh, yes," she smiled proudly, before adding, rather disconcertingly, "I just hope it's the right size."

Fortunately it was the right size and we got the wheel back together and back on the bike without any trouble. The woman then set about inflating it.

"I never know how much to put in," she gasped, pumping away.

"It should say on the side of the tyre," I replied, trying to see if I could find the information moulded into the rubber but the tyre was rocking about so much with her frantic inflations that it was impossible to read anything.

"Well, I can't put too much in can I?" she panted.

"Actually you can," I replied, recalling a recent incident.

My mountain bike had had a rear wheel puncture on my way home from work one rainy day, and when I had finally arrived home, having walked the last two miles, I was rather wet, rather cold and in rather a bad mood. Not inclined to stand in the rain any longer, I had pushed the bike into my kitchen and set about removing the wheel and repairing the puncture in the middle of the kitchen floor. With the tube patched and the wheel back together, I had grabbed my track pump from the shed and inflated the tyre effortlessly in a matter of seconds. I had done this so often that I knew without having to look at the tyre wall, just how much p.s.i. was needed to inflate the tyre.

Job done, and rain still coming down, I decided to leave the bike in the kitchen until the rain stopped. I made a cup of tea and then went upstairs for a shower. Coming back into the kitchen fifteen minutes later I was pleased to see the tyre was still inflated, well at least I knew I had got all the glass out. But as I set about making a meal I could hear an odd click-click-click noise. Where was it coming from? Kettle cooling? Oven warming up? Central heating on the blink? I wandered round the kitchen trying to pinpoint the source of the sound. It seemed to be the bike. Oh! I'd propped it against the door, maybe it was slowly slipping across the floor. I grabbed it by the handle bars and saddle and shoved it into a more stable position, then went back to peeling some carrots.

Click-click-click! Click-click-click! Click-click-click-click-click-click!!

"What the…?" I exclaimed swinging round towards the bike, preparing to have to catch it.

But the bike wasn't moving. So what was making the noise? I got down on all fours in front of the bike and began to carefully examine it. And that's when I spotted that the tyre was being forced off the rim by the bulging inner tube beneath it. The odd clicking sound was the tyre as it popped out in stages from

168

under the rim! My confidence at knowing the correct p.s.i. had been slightly misplaced. I realised with increasing panic, as I fumbled to undo the valve cap and let some air out of the tube, that I had got my numbers mixed up and inflated the mountain bike inner tube to the pressure that my road bike inner tube takes!

As my frantic finger finally pushed down on the top of the valve, the rush of air out of the over-pressurised tube nearly blew me across the kitchen. Cursing my own stupidity, I spent the next ten minutes removing the wheel, the tyre and the inner tube to check that everything was okay. Miraculously, the new patch was still holding and seemed completely unaffected by the excess pressure I had put it under. It was a lesson I did not forget.

Listening to my tale, the woman didn't know whether to laugh or sympathise. She stopped pumping and searched the tyre for the pressure information. But even having found it, without a pump that had a pressure gauge on it, the information was a bit useless.

"Test it with your thumb," I advised, and she duly did so.

Everything seemed fine. The tyre was firm and not too soft, and there were no odd clicking noises coming from it.

"Thank you so much," beamed the grateful woman. "Are you going far? Only you don't sound local."

"Just to North Queensferry, then I'm getting a train back to Newcastle."

"Oh," she considered. "You don't sound like you're from Newcastle."

"No, Burnley," I sighed.

"Oh, that explains it!" she said, seemingly enlightened.

Yes, it explains a lot, I thought.

We cycled together for a short distance, still chatting and still occasionally having to dodge broken glass. As we approached a junction of paths, the woman began to slow down.

"This is where I leave you," she explained. "I'm visiting my elderly mother, she lives down there. Thanks again for your help. Have a good trip. Oh, and by the way, you've got a smear of chain grease or something on your top lip."

"Oh. You're welcome. Thanks," I replied, scrubbing at my upper lip with the back of my glove.

Pleasant side roads carried me through Dalmeny and to the Forth Road Bridge which carried the A90, Scotland's equivalent of the A6 or the A1, north towards Inverness. The bridge was a dual carriageway, two lanes for each direction of traffic flow, separated by sturdy crash barriers. Another sturdy crash barrier separated the south bound traffic from a cycle lane, onto which signs directed me at Queensferry. The road signs suggested traffic was limited to fifty miles per hour, but it seemed to be travelling much faster than that as a constant street of trucks, lorries and cars travelled towards me.

Views from the bridge were spectacular, although the view west up the Firth of Forth was somewhat obscured by the bridge itself. I stopped to take some photos and lean against the rail, looking eastwards at the Forth Rail Bridge and beyond it out to the North Sea. Gulls floated on the air currents below me, their shrill cries nearly drowned out by the roar of traffic. As I watched, a train heading south crossed the rail bridge; it seemed to be travelling much slower than the traffic at my back. On the water, the wind was blowing up a series of white horses, and sailing boats bobbed about as they sailed under the spectacular curving arches of the rail bridge.

The two bridges spanning the Firth of Forth are very different, a contrast of engineering and construction methods separated by over seventy years. Standing around one kilometre apart, they both span the Firth at the narrowest point for several miles, engineering marvels that have superseded the ancient ferries that for centuries were the only means across this stretch of water.

The Forth Rail Bridge came first. The original design had been drawn up by a chap called Sir Thomas Bouch and work had just commenced to lay one of the first foundations when the powers that be suddenly began to have second thoughts. The reason for the sudden loss of confidence in Bouch's design was the fact that he had also designed the Tay Rail Bridge which, during a violent storm in 1879, had collapsed. Bad enough in itself. Made worse because a train had been on it at the time. More than seventy people had lost their lives.

So a couple of new engineers were brought in, their names were Sir John Fowler and Benjamin Baker. Work started on their design in 1882, and it was deliberately intended that it should appear strong to boost confidence following the Tay Bridge's collapse. It was built on the cantilever principle, with three towers supporting the weight and span of the bridge and carrying two rail tracks one hundred and fifty feet above high water level. The total height of the bridge is three hundred and sixty feet. In all it is over one and a half miles long, with the longest span being a third of a mile. The invoice total? £2.5 million. Nearly as many people died in its construction as were killed on the Tay Bridge disaster: over fifty men lost their lives building it. It was the first major structure in Britain to be made from the new wonder material, steel. Now a listed structure, it has needed constant maintenance ever since, and the phrase 'like painting the Forth Bridge' has become synonymous for a never ending task. However, it is actually a misconception that when painting has been completed at one end of the bridge it is time to start again at the other; although it does nevertheless keep a permanent team of workmen and engineers busy ensuring it is safe and well maintained.

The Forth Rail Bridge was completed in 1890 to much applause and celebration of another great British feat of engineering. At the opening ceremony, the last rivet, a gold plated one, was bashed into place by the Prince of Wales. I have to say, I think it might have been painted over, because despite having a good look, I couldn't see it when I travelled over on the train later that afternoon!

The Forth Road Bridge by comparison did not open until 1964 and cost considerably more; the bridge alone coming in at over £11 million with the extra works to realign roads etc. bringing the total up to nearer £20 million. In comparison to the Rail Bridge there was one statistic that had seen a reduction – the death toll of workmen on the project was seven, which is still seven too many. At the time the Road Bridge opened, it was the fourth longest suspension bridge in the world and the longest outside the United States. It has a total length of one and a half miles, with the span between the two towers measuring just over half a mile; the tops of the towers themselves stand over five hundred feet above the high water level. Those statistics alone were enough to make me feel dizzy. And when you consider the vast quantities and types of materials used in its construction, it can hardly be described as low carbon: 125,000 cubic metres of concrete and 39,000 tonnes of steel. And having watched films of the Tacoma Narrows Bridge collapse, I was inclined to think the Forth Road Bridge didn't look as reassuringly strong as its neighbour the Rail Bridge!

So perhaps it was time I stopped admiring the view and cycled across! The bridge rose up ahead of me, curving towards the centre of the span, before I enjoyed a descent on the second half of the bridge that led me onto a minor road into North Queensferry. And that was where I said goodbye to the Sustrans cycle route, I left it heading north and I headed for a tea room.

North Queensferry is a village sitting on the narrowest point of the Firth of Forth and is now dominated by the two great bridges that run above it on either side. On the southern bank of the Firth of Forth sits Queensferry, why it isn't called South Queensferry I don't know, but there you go. For centuries a ferry ran between the two settlements, the only means of crossing the water for miles around. The village takes its name from Saint Margaret, the wife of King (no, not David I) Malcolm III, and she it was who established the village here in order that pilgrims travelling to St. Andrews further to the north, could be assured of a regular ferry service. Margaret used the ferry between the two settlements quite regularly on her journeys between Edinburgh Castle and the then capital of Scotland, Dunfermline, just a few miles to the north. Sorry – one last mention and then that's it, I promise – after the death of his parents (Maggie and Malc) King David I granted the rights to provide a ferry here to the abbey, and although the abbey didn't last down the centuries, the ferries did, surviving for over eight hundred years.

The railway provided surprisingly little competition to the ferries and with the advent of the motor vehicle

the ferry service continued to be much in demand.
By the beginning of the 1960s it was estimated that
the ferry service was transporting over half a million
vehicles and some two million passengers each year.
It had reached the point where it simply could not
cope. The last commercial vehicle used the ferry the
day before Queen Elizabeth II opened the Forth Road
Bridge in 1964. Unlike her ancestor, there was no
golden rivet for her to whack into place.

North Queensferry might have lost its commercial
ferry service but for just a mere dot on the map it has
quite a lot going for it. There are hotels and guest
houses and tea rooms providing for tourists and
walkers using the Fife Coastal Path that has its
starting point in the village. On the eastern side of the
little headland there is a nature reserve. A large
aquarium pulls in tourists, particularly on wet days;
and there are plenty of old, interesting buildings in the
village to spend an afternoon strolling around. I
didn't have an afternoon, so I cycled quickly around
the village, taking in the sights from the saddle. I
cycled past Waterloo Well, with a Victorian iron
pump still in situ. The former Black Cat Inn, an inn
no longer, apparently has tunnels running from it
towards the sea, possibly used by smugglers in the old
days when there were heavy duties levied on tobacco
and spirits. The oldest remaining building in North
Queensferry is thought to be the fourteenth century
chapel dedicated to Saint John. Founded by Robert
the Bruce, it was abandoned at the time of the
reformation, then took a battering from
Parliamentarian troops during the Civil War. Most of
the houses lining the quiet main street are eighteenth

century, and I followed the street as it curved in a giant lazy letter 'm' through the village and down to the pier giving me views back across the water to the south. Although the village sprang up to serve the ferry and its passengers, this was not the only source of income for locals. There have been quarries in the area for hundreds of years. Dolerite, the same hard rock that Bamburgh Castle sits on, has been quarried here for centuries, providing paving stones for London and building stone for the docks in nearby Leith and further afield Liverpool. And if all that wasn't enough to tempt you to visit, North Queensferry is the home of Gordon Brown. I didn't see him.

As I turned round to head back to a tea room I had spotted, I noticed a fisherman leaning against the pier wall look at me and then do a double take. I thought no more of it: perhaps he just thought I'd lost my way off the cycle route. Arriving back at the cosy little tea room, I chained the bike outside and went in, taking off helmet and gloves as I went. I nearly bumped into a retired couple in the doorway, both of who seemed to give me odd, appraising looks as I apologised and held the door open for them. Maybe they weren't accustomed to polite cyclists round here, I thought.

There were a couple of empty tables and I chose the one giving me a wall (and radiator) to my back and a view of the room. I read through the menu, wondering if anything would be 'off' as it had been at Kelso. Having made my selection, I looked up and met the gaze of a teenage girl, sitting with a younger brother and her grandmother at a table on the other side of the room. I smiled, she glared and it was I who looked away first. At that moment the waitress approached to take my order, she too did a double take before scribbling my order on her pad and disappearing into the kitchen.

When I looked up the teenage girl was staring at me again. This time I didn't bother to smile. Then her grandmother looked at me and she too did a double take. Okay, I was beginning to wonder why I was attracting so many odd glances. Was my hair standing on end? I smoothed it down with my hands. Perhaps I had a bogie sitting on the end of my nose? I got out my hankie and gave it a good blow, then surreptitiously examined the hankie. No, nothing there. I put it down to my odd patterned sunburn and forgot about it.

The tea pot, milk, cup and saucer arrived. "Your jacket potato will be another couple of minutes," the waitress informed me, arranging the tea things in front of me and studiously avoiding looking at me.

"Okay, thanks," I replied.

That gave me just enough time to go and wash my hands and try to get rid of any remaining bits of chain grease and oil. I headed through the door in the corner of the room with a W.C. sign stuck on it and found myself facing two more doors: one male, one female. In the ladies I washed my hands and then checked in the mirror to see what state my hair, nose and sunburn were in.

"Eek! Julia, you're Hitler," I squeaked in shock. There, sitting under my nose was, not a bogie, but a narrow black smear of dirt. I had obviously failed to wipe the black mark off when I had tried earlier and I had just spent over an hour wandering about with a Hitler moustache!

I removed my glasses, rolled up my sleeves and got busy with plenty of soap and hot water but it wasn't really shifting the dirty mark. I had got used to the odd sunburn pattern, unruly hair was a way of life for me (with or without bathroom cleaner), but I really didn't want to go around for the rest of the day looking like Hitler! Experience has taught me that the best way to get rid of bike and chain oil and dirt is scalding hot water, washing up liquid and a scrubbing brush. But your average tea room toilets don't tend to supply those. In desperation I tried the nail brush that was sitting on the back of the sink. It hurt. But it did remove the mark, eventually. I returned to the tea room with a painfully red upper lip, just as my jacket potato with tuna mayonnaise and side salad arrived.

"Thank you," I said to the waitress.

"You're welcome," she smiled, giving me another odd glance as she spotted my red raw moustache.

Ten minutes later she returned to clear the empty plate, asking, "Can I get you anything else?"

"Yes, please could I have the apple pie," I asked, having spotted it on the specials board.

"Yes certainly," she replied. She noted it down on her pad and glancing again at my red and stinging top lip, added: "Would you like some cream with that?"

With my mind still on my red raw face, I replied, "No thanks, I've got some Vaseline in my bag."

Clearly thinking I was bonkers she hurried off. It wasn't until she'd gone that I realised what she had meant.

By the time I had eaten my apple pie, which had come with cream, and drank my tea, it was time to go. I paid the bill and left the tea room, with the teenage girl still staring at me as I went. I was overcome with a childish impulse to stick my tongue out at her but refrained, she clearly already thought I was a big enough idiot.

I cycled up the hill to the railway station and wheeled the bike onto the platform. A mural comprising of thousands of mosaic tiles covered one wall, made in part by local school children it had been created to mark the centenary of the opening of the station. I had just ten minutes to wait for my train and stood there looking at the mural, checking my watch and removing the panniers from the bike.

When the train arrived a friendly guard helped me load the bike onto the train. I fastened the lock through the rear wheel and the frame, just in case anyone was tempted to steal a dirty, sheep poo adorned hybrid, and then, carrying the panniers, went to find my seat in one of the middle carriages. The

179

train set off on time and I watched Edinburgh and the Borders, Berwick-upon-Tweed and the east coast whizzing past in a few hours. Just south of Berwick I watched as the grey sea and the wheeling gulls passed in a blur, then I caught a high speed glimpse of a cyclist standing waiting to cross the line just as I had done a few days ago.

It began raining long before the train drew into the main railway station at Newcastle. I clambered out onto the platform, battling with panniers and bicycle amid a thronging crowd of tea time commuters. Outside the station I swapped my maps round, now I was back on the Coast and Castles map, on the first part of it.

I had cycled this part before, as it was the same as the ending of the Sea to Sea Cycle Route which I had completed the previous year with a friend, so I was feeling confident of not getting lost. Yes, well. Straight out of the railway station, into busy traffic and I found myself lost. 'Start and finish at Newcastle Station' said a notation on my map, so it should have been simple! There should have been cycle route signs! So why couldn't I see any? I cycled round in a circle and ended up back at the station. In the end I just cycled down the nearest hill and onto the riverside path. The rain was bouncing off the surface of the river, and the old Baltic Flour Mill seemed to have a cloud base sitting on top of it. It all looked very grey.

Much has been done in recent years to redevelop Newcastle and its riverside. The old industries of coal, steel and shipbuilding are long gone. And so is the Roman fort at Wallsend. The rain, by now lashing down and dripping off my helmet, chin and cagoule, did not add to my appreciation of the redevelopment along the north bank of the Tyne, mostly because I couldn't see very much. My glasses were steaming up and running with water and my raw upper lip was stinging. Fortunately I had just fourteen miles to cycle back to the car at Whitley Bay but the first few of those miles, cycled in the heavy rain, seemed to drag on interminably.

I passed Jarrow on the south side of the river, the Tyne pedestrian and cycle tunnel, old abandoned warehouses, derelict sites awaiting redevelopment and several shopping trolleys. By the time I reached a sign pointing to the North Sea ferry terminal, I was feeling rather sorry for myself, what a soggy end to what had been a most enjoyable cycling trip. 'Wet and Wild' said the next sign I saw.

"Yes I am!" I concurred.

As I cycled into the quiet streets of Tynemouth, and then onto traffic-free paths out towards the priory and castle on the headland, the rain suddenly stopped and a strong wind sprang up, lifting the clouds and blowing them to Denmark. A weak sun began to gain strength and slowly reassert itself, making the wet pavements shine and reflecting in the puddles of rainwater that collected along the cycle track.

The ruins perched on the headland are all that remain of Tynemouth Priory and Castle. Built in the eleventh century, they replaced the earlier monastery which was sacked by invading Danes in the seventh century. Before that there had been Iron Age settlements there. Tynemouth Castle had been fortified and used by several English Kings as a base for their skirmishes into Scotland and the Borders. Like so many places I had cycled through in the last few days, Tynemouth had a long and complicated history of settlement, war, religion and eventually peace. Today Tynemouth is a rather nice, genteel commuter town for Newcastle and a pleasant seaside resort. Traditional seaside holidaymakers still come with their buckets and spades and enjoy Longsands Beach, voted one of the best in Europe. Tynemouth, unlike Whitley Bay, does not specialise in stag and hen parties; I saw not a single blonde wig, purple high heel or under-dressed groom-to-be!

I stopped for a drink and a rest overlooking the beach. The tide was on its way back in and waves were lapping around the feet of a gaggle of sandcastles of all shapes and sizes. Despite the wet weather, the British holiday maker could obviously not be deterred from entering into the seaside spirit. Most of the engineers responsible had packed up their buckets and spades and gone home, but one lone little figure was still there, waving a bright yellow spade around as if commanding the sea to go back and spare his sandcastle. Suddenly I heard a defiant wail as a larger wave washed up to engulf his castle and his wellies, sweeping him off his feet and depositing him on top of the amorphous remains of his creation. His dad dashed back down the beach to rescue him, carrying him away in tears. Is that how the English and Scots felt when they saw their own north eastern castles besieged by opposing armies? From all I had seen of the ancient castle ruins in the last few days, it seemed they had often been no more impregnable than sand on a beach.

By the time I returned to my car, just a couple of miles further north along the coast, the sun had dried my leggings and my cagoule, although my trainers will still very damp. I cycled up to the B&B half expecting to see my car had been damaged or adorned with wigs but it was sitting there unharmed and exactly as I had left it. I climbed off the bike, and checked the cycle computer: 260 miles, average speed 12.6 miles per hour, maximum speed 33.5 miles per hour, calories used 3.

"Oh, come on!" I'm, no maths genius, but even I know that was one calculation I couldn't believe.

I took the panniers and the front wheel off the bike and loaded everything into the car. Then loaded myself behind the wheel and prayed the car would start, at ten years old it could be temperamental on occasion, I knew how it felt. It started first time and I carefully reversed off the drive and drove back down to the sea front. Parking by the promenade, I checked no one was about before swiftly changing my cycling gear for jeans and jumper and my soggy trainers and socks for clean, dry ones that I had left in the car.

Before I drove home that evening there was just one more thing to do: get some food! But not fish and chips! Instead I food a kebab shop which looked clean and certainly smelt tempting. Sitting in the car, watching the sun go down inland of the Spanish City, I munched my way through chicken kebab with salad and garlic sauce and a portion of salt and vinegar enriched chips. This time there would be nothing left to throw to the seagulls.

I was just getting out of the car to put the empty food wrappers in a nearby bin, when I heard a yell.

"Hello, darling!"

Turning, I was confronted by a young man dressed in purple high heels, a leopard print top that barely concealed his hairy chest, black fishnet stockings, suspenders, X-rated mini skirt that could easily have been mistaken for a belt, lots of badly applied makeup and the ubiquitous blonde wig. Several equally sartorial young men were a little further behind him and heading my way.

"Jesus," I blurted inadvertently.

"No, Jamie," he replied in earnest, swaying slightly. That might have been due to the heels or the alcohol, I wasn't sure but I knew both things had the same effect on me! "I'm getting married tomorrow. How about a kiss? Whaddaya say?"

After all I'd just experienced, there was really only one thing I could say.

"On yer bike!"

Equipment List

bicycle

multi tool

pump

2 inner tubes
top
puncture repair kit

water bottle
jacket
map case

lock

maps
knickers
helmet

gloves

panniers

toiletries

pyjamas

first aid kit

handkerchief

sunglasses

paperback

pen

purse

mobile phone

digital camera

teabags

chocolate

trainers

cycling leggings

cycling shorts

high vis cycling

fleece jumper

waterproof

sandals

2 pairs of socks

2 pairs of

2 bras

T-shirt

trousers

Looking at the list of clothing, there does not seem to be much at all. But experience has shown you actually need very little clothing when travelling in spring and summer - in even Britain! Although on this journey I could have saved myself the extra weight and left my sunglasses at home.

The blouse, trousers and one set of underwear are worn in the evenings. The clothes worn whilst cycling are washed and dried each evening. The underwear from the evening is worn for cycling the next day and then hand washed, by doing this I always have a clean set of underwear. It is rare to be cold enough whilst cycling to ever need both fleece jumper and cagoule, and so these items of clothing remain clean enough to be used in the evenings.

About the Rider

Born in 1967, I grew up before the advent of mountain bikes and stunt bikes and bikes with no saddles; BMXs were just beginning to cause a stir as I entered my teens. Through my formative years bikes were either the drop handle bar variety or the sit up and beg with a basket on the front type. Suspension was something only motor vehicles had and most bikes either had one gear or Sturmey Archer hub gears, unless they were the slick-tyred, narrow-saddled racing bikes with gear shifters on the down tubes. There were no Barbie or Action Man or Fireman Sam cycles. And from personal experience I was under the impression that all bikes had one type of valve in the front tyre and another in the rear. Oh how times have changed! Now there seems to be more engineering in a bicycle than your average family car, with a price tag to match.

My first memory of cycling involves a tricycle, a length of rope and my mum. I was in the local park, sitting on a little tricycle, attached to the handlebars of which was the rope, with my mum attached to the other end. I suppose I would have been three or four years old. I think the idea was I would pedal and mum would assist on the gradients. Well, that was mum's idea. I can distinctly remember her crossly telling me I was supposed to be pedalling.

My next memory is of my dad teaching me to ride a borrowed bicycle in another local park. He ran along behind, maintaining my balance by holding onto the rear of the bike whilst I cycled erratically across the playground. Either his technique was good or my balance was superb, I tend to think it was the former, because suddenly I realised the sound of his voice encouraging me on was becoming fainter: he had let go. I wobbled to a stop to discover I had cycled quite a distance unaided. That one lesson, with a brilliant, patient teacher, was all it took. From then on I rode any friend's bike I could cadge, borrow or pinch while their backs were turned.

It was probably a couple of years before I got a bike of my own: a second hand, yellow, fixed gear, fat-tyred machine which I loved. It arrived at Christmas, shrouded in a sheet; I had asked for a rocking horse in the hope of playing cowboys and Indians and cops and robbers, never believing I would actually get one. The bike was a much better present: I could still play those games but with the added excitement of fresh air, punctures and grazed palms.

Choppers had just arrived on the market and were all the rage with their odd-sized wheels, stick shift gear knob on the cross bar, swept back handlebars and long stylish saddle. My dad told me mine was a Chipper and I believed him wholeheartedly and went around telling all my friends, receiving much derision in the process. But I didn't care, I loved that bike. I cycled round the quiet side streets and in the park, mum never allowed me to go on the main roads; even though they were much quieter then than they are now, she worried. (She still does, and I'm still not allowed on the main roads!) And then disaster struck on the evening before I was due to take my cycling proficiency test at junior school: I was pedalling up my steep front street, standing up on the pedals and leaning on the handlebars, when without warning the handlebars sheared off. My treasured bike was beyond repair. The proficiency test went out the window and the bike went out with the rubbish. It was never replaced.

But cycling still tempted me and on every occasion I could I begged 'goes' on friends', and sometimes strangers', bikes. Bike shops and full bicycle racks held a fascination that still exists today. One boyfriend even offered to build me a bike, but I'm still waiting. I would borrow his drop handlebar road bike and take off round the block, but he was forever fiddling with it, modifying it, changing things. The last time I borrowed it he had swapped the brakes round, a modification I only became aware of when I applied what the previous week had been the rear brake only to find myself flying gracelessly over the handlebars on a busy main road. I came to surrounded by bits of bike and with my thigh firmly wedged in the curving drop handle bars. It was a long time before I got on a bike again.

I grew up, got a few A levels, got a job and then another and got married (but we all make mistakes), got a couple of cats and even got a bike with Sturmey Archer gears. But hilly east Lancashire isn't the sort of place for a bike with only three gears and our relationship was brief. Then we moved to a cottage in an even hillier bit of east Lancashire and all thoughts of bicycles went out of my head, I walked regularly and swam often and that was all the exercise I needed.

But then, on a whim, I bought a hybrid. It had twenty-one gears and a pannier rack, and it lived in our cramped kitchen for a couple of years where I was forever catching my sleeve on the handle bars as I was going past with a cup of tea and having to mop the floor as a result. Eventually, fed up of whacking my ankles on the pedals, I bought a shed. The bike lived in the shed, coming out nearly every day to take me to work.

In September 2001 I did my first cycling holiday with a friend: the Sea to Sea. I'd got the bug. From then on there was no stopping me! The following spring I cycled the Coast and Castles route on my own – the one you've just read about – and there was plenty more to come. And plenty more to write about!

Before the cycling holidays there had been walking holidays, long distance National Trails in England and Wales. I had already written several books about my walking adventures and so it seemed only natural to write about my mishaps in the saddle. The walks, the rides and the resulting books just kept on coming…

By the Same Author:

Cycling Across England
© Julia R May 2012
https://tinyurl.com/yc62pful

Two women, two bikes, no backup on a Sea to Sea adventure.

At the beginning of the twenty-first century two friends set off to cycle from coast to coast across England. For one, it was to be the first of many long distance cycle rides.

Cycling Across England is an account of the fun, the food, the mountains, the moorlands and the mathematics the two friends encountered along the way. From the Irish Sea, through the mountains of Cumbria and the Pennine uplands they travelled through a landscape of contrasts to finish their journey in the industrial northeast on the North Sea coast. Broken glass, slugs and arduous ascents were relieved by blackberries, an excess of pizza and delightful descents. Join them as they cycle across England on this iconic ride.

I've Cycled Through There
© Julia R May 2012
https://tinyurl.com/ybxf3gfj

That strangest of traveller, the lone female, is at it again. This time cycling through the heart of England from Bath to London to her home in Lancashire. For such a small country England was proving to be a land of contrasts and surprises; from the leafy lanes of Berkshire to the bleak moorlands of the north, spectacular scenery and post-industrial mill towns, dead divas and murderous mad men.

Throughout the six hundred mile cycle ride there was much that was quintessentially English: Georgian architecture and thatched cottages, William Shakespeare and Samuel Johnson, Bath buns and Yorkshire pudding, canals and Roman roads, Magna Carta and the Houses of Parliament, oh, and Maharajah's Wells and teams of huskies!

Share the experience, the food, the fun and the frustrations. Funny and factual by turns, this is a true account of a cycle journey home through the heart of England.

Walking with Hadrian
© Julia R May 2012
https://tinyurl.com/y9929ggz

A walk through time and fog along Hadrian's Wall.

Built almost two thousand years ago on the orders of the Emperor Hadrian and marking the northern-most boundary of the Roman Empire, Hadrian's Wall is one of Britain's most enduring ancient monuments and a UNESCO World Heritage Site. In 2003 a footpath following the line of the Wall was designated as a National Trail running 84 miles across England from the Solway Firth to the North Sea. Since then walkers have been coming to enjoy this long distance path in the wild landscape of northern England, and a few years later inadvertently choosing the foggiest week she could, Julia finally got round to walking the Wall.

Factual and funny by turns, 'Walking with Hadrian' is an accurate account of the history, culture, scenery and wildlife of Hadrian's Wall Path. Battling fog, maps, social networking and the encroaching perils of middle age, the author has added another book to her collection of traveller's tales.

A Week in Provence
© Julia R May 2014
https://tinyurl.com/y7pruz4x

A much needed autumn break walking in the Verdon Gorge region of Provence turns into a fraught lesson in how not to speak French as the author gets to grips with the language of love, romance and strange combinations of Cs, Qs, apostrophes and genders. Written with her by now trademark self-deprecating humour, this, the author's tenth travelogue, recounts the beauty, the peace and the quieter way of life to be found walking in idyllic rural France.

Never a successful student of languages, but believing you ought to try, Julia displays an enthusiastic if dreadful grasp (or should that be stranglehold?) of the French language as the week unfolds. Whilst coping with a lack of underpants, some rather smelly food and the intricacies of French, A Week in Provence tells of the walks walked, the food eaten, the language butchered and the stretched patience of her long suffering partner as they embark on a walking holiday in south east France.

Bicycles, Boats and Bagpipes
© Julia R May 2014
https://tinyurl.com/y7hrnokp

Having cycled the length and breadth of the British
mainland, it was time for a change. After seeing a
little blue cycle route sign on the west coast of
Scotland, Julia was struck with inspiration. The
islands of the Outer Hebrides beckoned. There was
just one problem, her boyfriend wanted to go too!
Looking on the bright side he could be responsible for
navigating and could take most of the luggage. Well,
that was the plan. Little did she realise that with her
boyfriend there also came his smelly footwear and
holey cycling leggings.

Bicycles, Boats and Bagpipes is a detailed and often
amusing account of a 500 mile cycle journey through
the beautiful and remote islands of the Outer Hebrides
and along the mountainous northwest coast of the
Scottish mainland.

But it wasn't all about the cycling; there were the rare
flower-rich machairs of the Western Isles, idyllic
white sandy beaches, blue seas, wild moorland and
ancient historic sites to explore. Wildlife to watch.
Ferries to sail. Cake to eat and tea to drink. And
throughout the trip the experience of isolated
communities going about their daily lives, such a
contrast from the hustle and bustle of home.

Bicycles, Beer and Black Forest Gateau
© Julia R May 2016
https://tinyurl.com/yctr5bbg

Not many people would consider cycling hundreds miles through Europe to be a relaxing holiday. Mike certainly didn't. But Julia did, she was peculiar that way. There was a challenge to be had in following the River Rhine from its source high in the Swiss Alps, through Germany, France and the Netherlands to the North Sea. But if Mike could not be convinced by mention of the varied scenery, the cultural diversity and the cake, what would change his mind? Finally it was mention of the hundreds of breweries in Germany that convinced him. Who knew, it might turn out to be very relaxing after all?

But as the couple were to discover, cycling on the continent can be very different to cycling in Britain. It was not just the language that would prove difficult to get to grips with, the rules of the road, the navigation, the continental heat and the alpine thunderstorms would test their patience as would tractor drivers and mosquitoes. But most challenging of all would be two weeks without a proper cup of tea. Would beer, gateaux and chocolate be enough to compensate?

Dawdling Through The Dales
© Julia R May 2018
https://tinyurl.com/y8kew292

The Dales Way long distance footpath runs for over eighty miles from Ilkley to Bowness-on-Windermere, encompassing the beautiful scenery of North Yorkshire and Cumbria and two National Parks. It is a varied walk of ever-changing scenery of lush river valleys, limestone pavements, moorland and mountains, and one undertaken by thousands of walkers every year.

When two friends decided to walk the Dales Way over a series of weekends they expected to complete it within a year, but life got in the way. For one of them, the Dales Way would remain an uncompleted long distance footpath.

With details of the scenery, the natural history and anecdotes about the walk, this book will give you a true flavour of walking this often overlooked yet delightful footpath. Light hearted but also darker at times, Dawdling through the Dales, like all of Julia's books, will make you laugh, but it might also make you cry. It is a true tale of walking, divorce, betrayal, depression and enduring friendship.

Cycling Through a Foreign Field
© Julia R May 2018
https://tinyurl.com/yc3rv2y7

In an overheated room in a sheltered housing complex in Burnley there is a small, carved wooden box. The box is a depository for memories, half remembered or forgotten entirely. Inside this box are two life times of old photographs, some sepia, some black and white, known and unknown ancestors; and laid carefully on top of them all sits a newspaper clipping, faded and torn at the edges, over one hundred years old now.

The clipping was taken from the Burnley Express which in 1916 was running a regular feature of Burnley families and the contributions they were making to the First World War. The clipping shows eight head and shoulder photographs of mother and father and six of their sons. One son is in a reserved occupation, one son is too young to fight. The other four sons are in uniform, serving soldiers in the Great War.

The occupant of this hot, stuffy little room and keeper of this box of memories is a lady in her late eighties, frail now and suffering from Alzheimer's Disease, her memory is fading like the contents of the box. She is my mother, Rose. The youngest son in the old newspaper clipping is her father.

In spring 2018 my partner and I set out to cycle the battlefields of Flanders and The Somme; to retrace our forefathers' footsteps and to find out a little of where they served, the conditions they endured and

198

what had become of them during the First World War.

By the same author but written under her previous name:

My Feet and Other Animals
© Julia R Merrifield 2003
https://tinyurl.com/y98fnuqx

When two friends planned a long distance walk on England's South West Coast Path they thought the toughest challenge would be the walking itself. But the biggest obstacles to be overcome were not the 630 miles of footpaths, or the soaring ascents and descents of the cliffs. They were the unforeseen factors that cannot be planned for but which transform a journey into an adventure. Factors such as a torn calf muscle, recalcitrant underwear, two days of torrential rain and gales, two weeks of the hottest July temperatures for years, high tech equipment designed to help but determined to hinder, the capriciousness of public transport and a host of B&Bs all competing for the title of Worst Accommodation in the West.

Walking Pembrokeshire with a Fruitcake
© Julia R Merrifield 2004
https://tinyurl.com/ycnuhgev

Two friends deliberated where to choose for their next walking holiday. How about somewhere different? How about somewhere exotic? How about somewhere foreign? How about Wales? But with countless people advising them where to walk that summer and with neither of them speaking a word of Welsh, had they made the right decision? On a hot August day they set off to walk the 180 miles of the Pembrokeshire Coast Path, starting from somewhere unpronounceable and finishing at a little place called Amroth, passing on the way lots more places they would struggle to enunciate.

Wales, a proud land with a proud past; a land steeped in history, a land of myths and magic, castles and cromlechs, dragons and double consonants, male voice choirs and Aled Jones. Follow their adventures as they search for ice cream vans and a Welsh dictionary.

Pedals, Panniers and Punctures
© Julia R Merrifield 2005

One woman, one bike, no backup and 1477 miles on a unique End to End adventure.

Since when did cycle touring become an extreme sport? Since it involved travelling by train. When one woman, more accustomed to long distance footpaths than long distance cycle rides, set out to cycle from Land's End to John o'Groats the first obstacle she faced was getting to the start. Between the start of her journey and the finish, 1477 miles later, she encountered not only ups and downs of terrain but mental and physical highs and lows as well.

Cycling the End to End is so much more than just sitting on something no bigger than, and as hard as, the sole plate of an iron and pedalling, as Julia was to discover. Every experience seemed to be about extremes: Cornish hills, Cheshire plains, busy Devon lanes, empty highland roads, downpours, droughts, smooth cycle tracks, hazardous cattle grids, psychedelic B&Bs and homely hostels. And when the terrain and the weather weren't against her the wildlife was: terrorising Labradors, formation herding sheep dogs, kamikaze squirrels, plagues of midges and road-senseless sheep.

With no backup, and just a bike and a puncture repair kit for company, that strangest of traveller, the lone female, set off to tackle the ultimate British cycle ride. If only she had got a pound for every time someone told her it was all downhill the other way she could have bought a lot more chocolate. As it was, sustained by copious quantities of tea and as much chocolate as she could carry she finally reached her wet and windswept goal.

Walking with Offa
© Julia R Merrifield 2006
https://tinyurl.com/yd73j3q8

Ever heard of a bloke called Offa? King of Mercia,
he instigated the building of a defensive dyke.
Twelve centuries later a long distance path was laid
out, roughly following the line of Offa's Dyke, and
thirty years later still two friends set out to walk it.

How difficult could it be, walking from one end of
Wales to the other? Loaded down with maps, guide
books and global positioning systems they were soon
to find out and only five minutes after leaving
Chepstow were monumentally lost! Soon they were
enjoying the scenery, watching the wildlife and
overdosing on dried apricots. Staying in haunted
English castles and heavenly Welsh guest houses they
made their way north.

Find me on Facebook:

For excerpts from my books, photos and more information.

Julia R May Books on Kindle & Kobo

https://www.facebook.com/JuliaRMayBooksOnKindle?ref_type=bookmark

If you like what I do – let people know. If you don't – shh! ☺